first
Days on
the JOB

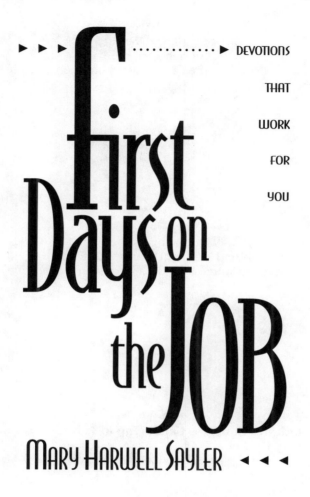

DEVOTIONS
THAT
WORK
FOR
YOU

First Days on the JOB

MARY HARWELL SAYLER

BROADMAN
& HOLMAN
PUBLISHERS

Nashville, Tennessee

4253-73
0-8054-5373-3

Dewey Decimal Classification: 242
Subject Heading: Devotional Literature
Library of Congress Card Catalog Number: 94-3708

Library of Congress Cataloging-in-Publication Data
Sayler, Mary Harwell.
    First days on the job : devotions that work for you / Mary Har-
well Sayler.
        p.   cm.
    ISBN 0-8054-5373-3
    1. Work—Religious aspects—Christianity—Prayer-books and
devotions—English.   2. Young adults—Prayer-books and devotions—Christianity.   3. Devotional calendars.   I. Title.

BV4593.S28   1994
242'.2—dc20

                                                        94-3708
                                                        CIP

This book is dedicated
with love and admiration
to my sister, Marcia Anne Harwell,
whose hard work now brings her
to the start of a blessed career;
to my children, Greg, Paige, and Adam,
who presently seek their life's work,
and to my younger siblings,
Kay, Mark, and Keith,
who learned well from our parents
the importance of doing work we like.
Thanks also to the excellent staff
at Broadman & Holman Publishers,
whose attention to detail brings such
professionalism to Christian publishing,
and to Sandy Brooks for taking on
Christian Writers Fellowship International
and freeing me to do the work God gave me:
teaching other Christian writers and poets—
and writing again myself!

May God bless them—
and you—
as you begin your first days on the job!

As you begin your first days of full-time employment, you'll get off to a great start by employing yourself in the reading of God's Word! This devotional book will help you apply Scripture to the typical on-the-job situations you'll encounter. If something unusual or confusing arises, you can find the answers you need by researching that particular topic in the version of the Bible *you most like to read.*

There are many fine versions from which to choose, such as *The Amplified Bible, New King James Version, New Jerusalem Bible, New American Bible, New American Standard, Revised English Bible,* and *The Bible In Today's English* (also known as the *Good News Bible.*) in this book, Scriptures come from the Bible versions frequently read in worship services or in study groups of all denominations. These translations are shown as follows:

KJV = *King James Version*

NCV = Scriptures quoted from *The Youth Bible, New Century Version,* copyright © 1991 by Word Publishing, Dallas, Texas 75039. Used by permission.

Nothing replaces Bible reading! This book isn't meant to substitute God's Word but to show its relevance to you and your circumstances as you start your first days on the job. To get off to a blessed start, begin having regular devotions each morning or evening, depending on which is better for you. Set aside time to read the Bible, pray, and keep a journal (using the ruled pages in the back of this book or a separate notebook), to help you focus your prayers and record your thoughts, feelings, and the events of each new day.

If you would like for me to pray for you as you start work, drop me a note in care of Broadman & Holman Publishers, 127 Ninth Avenue North, Nashville, TN 37234. Please enclose an SASE (self-addressed stamped envelope) if you'd like a response. Thanks. The Lord be with you always in Christ's name.

▶ ▶ ▶ **Day 1** ◀ ◀ ◀

*You may work and get everything
done during six days each week,
but the seventh day is a day of rest to
honor the Lord your God.
On that day no one may do any
work: not you, your son or daughter,
your male or female slaves, . . .
or any of your animals.*

(Deuteronomy 5:13–14, NCV)

All right! You got the job! Congratulations! You're now employed. So, while you still have time to think, think about taking a break!

Few people plan their time off when they haven't even begun to work! But, before you get involved in your new job, you probably want to know what's expected of you, right? For example, your new employer will expect you to arrive on time and reasonably rested, so you're *able* to do a full day's work for the agreed-upon wage. Well, as you enter the work-world, God also has certain expectations.

People might not think too much about it, but God's Word clearly says what He expects: Within six working days, He wants you to take care of everything you need to do for that week. On the seventh day, rest—period. That's it! No up-and-over-time allowed!

Isn't that terrific? God is the first Equal Opportunity Employer! Not only does His fair policy fit the person who's starting at minimum wage (or no wage!), it adjusts up the scale to fit heads of big corporations. Regardless of status, you're to work six days and then rest. Work six days and then rest. Work six. Rest one.

Apparently, God wants no one to think, "Oh, that doesn't apply to *me!*" So He even included kids, animals, and non-paid workers! Why? God Himself took a break and knows the value of resting. Besides, trying to outdo God is a prideful sin, and the wages of that is working oneself to death!

So, as you start your new job, keep in mind that God gives everyone an equitable twenty-four-hour day, six days a week to do the work that's needed. Most employers will only expect you to spend forty of those hours at work. Some may expect thirty to sixty. But surely no employer on earth—and certainly no Employer in heaven—will expect you on the job for the 144 hours found in a six-day workweek! Now that really would be a full-time job!

Prayer: Heavenly Father, thank You for setting the same job standards for everyone. Help me to use the time You've given me to do my work and enjoy the rest You bring in Jesus' name.

Journaling with God: To get off to a good start at work, begin a daily devotional time of Bible reading and journaling with God. In the space provided, record any expectations you have placed on yourself about working full-time. Then, ask God to clarify *His* expectations, listening to the thoughts He brings to your mind—and adjusting your view of work to His!

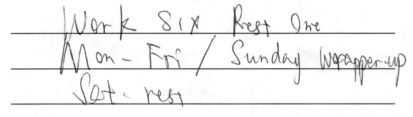

Work Six Rest One
Mon - Fri / Sunday wrapper up
Sat - rest

*The Lord God took the man
and put him in the Garden of Eden
to work it and take care of it.*

(Genesis 2:15, NIV)

Have you filled out enough company forms to wallpaper The White House? Have you answered more questions than you'd need on a game show to win a round-trip ticket to Tibet?

Processing paperwork is just part of your employer's job to meet government regulations and (of major importance!) to get you on the payroll. Once that's done, hallelujah! You're officially employed!

So here's your first official, post-employment question: Ready? What's the very first job God hired mankind to do? (Hint: you'll find the answer at the top of this page!) Easy, huh? Mankind's first job is taking care of God's creations.

Since you got that right, it's only fair to give you a question-asking turn. So, here are a couple of *answers* for you to *question*: 1. The first job opening always stays open! (When you have more time, think about that! However, the main point comes next.) 2. Before anyone ever thought of sinning, *God gave people work to do.*

In the beginning of your first days on the job, you'll be blessed to have this God-given principle clearly in mind: The Lord doesn't see work as a *punishment* but as a *privilege.*

In the perfect world He created, God gave people jobs! Even now, He involves you in His creation. He includes you in His work.

Whether you work in an air-conditioned car, a freezing office, a floral hot-house, a hot toll booth, or a hot dog stand on a glacier, God's command has not changed. He has put you in your own job environment—to work it and take care of it—for as long as you remain in that perfectly lovely spot!

Prayer: Dear Creator, God, I praise You for Your creation. In the beginning, the whole world was absolutely perfect, and, before I start this job, it's perfect, too. I haven't made any mistakes yet! Please help me to do a good job and take care of the work You've given me in Jesus' name.

Journaling with God: In the very beginning of your job, confess your failure! Ask God to bring to mind any past mistakes presently concerning you or affecting future work. Write your thoughts below, leaving room for God's Word of forgiveness.

_____

_____

_____

_____

_____

_____

*If so be that being clothed
we shall not be found naked.*

(2 Corinthians 5:3, KJV)

"Oh, no! What am I going to wear?"

Unless you have a standard uniform issued to you, you'll wonder what's appropriate to wear to work. Perhaps you have had an opportunity to see other employees in the workplace during your interviews. If not, try to observe as people come and go to their jobs. See if you *really* need to throw out your whole wardrobe or if you just think you do!

Chances are you have *something* in your closet that will be appropriate for work—at least until you get a paycheck or two. However, if not a stitch of your wardrobe is work-able but the buttons, that's the place to start! (Maybe they'll fit an outfit found in a second-hand clothing store.)

You might consider swapping clothes with a friend who's your size or larger. In desperation borrow. Also, shop for sales to find reasonable prices on what you need. As you begin to have a regular income, allow yourself a clothing allowance. But, whatever you do, don't expect your wardrobe to cover you up!

Even in the shower, your body clothes your soul and spirit. Plain packaging or fancy, the wondrous part of you can not be seen by human eyes or microscopic tests. Your

soul (attitudes, personality) makes you unique. Your spirit (good humor, kindness, love) makes you very well-dressed!

Although your spiritual self is completely invisible, it's highly visible too. It's unseen but can't be hidden with multiple layers of coats, vests, or undies! No suit of armor or porcupine quills will protect you either. No matter what you wear, eventually you'll be *seen-through* by other people at work who make it their job to know you.

Prayer: Dear God, I'd just as soon people not know some things about me! Are those the very things I need to talk about with You? Help me to offer You any displeasing parts of me in the forgiveness of Christ's name.

Journaling with God: With God's help, bring your hidden self to Him for forgiveness as you journal in the space below.

_____

_____

_____

_____

_____

_____

_____

_____

_____

In the same way,
you who are younger
must accept the authority
of the elders.
And all of you must clothe yourselves
with humility in your dealings
with one another,
for "God opposes the proud,
but gives grace to the humble."

(1 Peter 5:5, NRSV)

Do your work clothes come with designer labels? Most jobs need warning labels that read: Caution! Lack of humility wears out the fabric of your character (not to mention your welcome at work!).

Before you clock in each day, check any attitudes that could be clothed with pride. For example, if you've ever had the thought, "I deserve a much better job than this," you may be right. But, unfortunately, that smudge of arrogance could mar your chances of getting one!

Especially during these first days on the job, the most important outfit in your closet is humility. And if getting humility over your head is a tight squeeze, talk with God about that. Or if humility hangs on you like a big bag of potatoes, you might get sacked! Ask God to dress you in the humble self-worth that comes from knowing Him.

As you get well-clothed in humility, color your thoughts with care. Overdoing it would be like putting on heavy makeup or drowning yourself in after-shave. Don't be artificial; be real! Remind yourself that you're new in this job and, therefore, have a lot to learn. Then, comb out any negative thoughts and make up your mind to face your

employer and other experienced workers with the respect they deserve for knowing their jobs well.

Prayer: Dear God, thank You for the job You've given to me. Help me to let go of any feelings of pride or thoughts of worthlessness, so I'm able to wear a humble spirit that does not bag, sag, or chafe. Help me to receive the instructions I'm given about my new job so I can learn quickly and do the work well in Jesus' name.

Journaling with God: How do you feel about your new job? Talk with God about it. Then listen to His response. This may come to you in a new thought or a larger view of your work than you'd previously considered.

_____

_____

_____

_____

_____

_____

_____

_____

_____

_____

_____

▶ ▶ ▶ **Day**
5
◀ ◀ ◀

*Here is a call for the endurance
of the saints, those who keep
the commandments of God
and hold fast
to the faith of Jesus.*

(Revelation 14:12, NRSV)

The first week of a new job can be rough! You may have spent years preparing for a career only to find yourself in a low-entry position. Or perhaps you've tortured yourself with *if only's*: "If only I'd followed my parents' advice . . . ," "If only I'd studied more on Tuesdays. . . ," "If only I'd been born big, bold, beautiful, and bright. . . ."

Besides the torment of regret, you might feel tortured by the work itself or the conditions around you. For example, if you spent years bench-pressing books, a job that requires physical strength might make your muscles ache until you build up more endurance. Or if you're used to taking the lead, you may be exhausted by keeping step with an unsure-footed manager.

If you don't like being on a low rung of the ladder or have a crick in your neck trying to look up, just step to a higher view! Here's the big, bold, beautiful, and bright picture: You're doing *the* work God gave you to do *for now*.

You did ask Him about this job *before* you accepted it, right? If not, oops! Step back to the ground floor and on your knees! Ask God what He thinks of this work and whether it pleases Him.

If you're doing just what you've been given at this particular time in your life, you might not like it much! But you will have a sense of peace about your job.

You'll know you don't need to worry about the past, present, or future. You don't need to wonder if you'll ever be trusted to do bigger, better, bolder, brighter, or more beautiful things! You will know that *God* can be trusted not to drop you below the ground floor as you hold on, fast, to Him!

Prayer: Heavenly Father, help me to overcome my fears in facing what's new and find the strength to endure adjustments to full-time work. Thank You for my job and for the assurance that You hold onto me tightly in Jesus' name.

Journaling with God: In the space below, list specific fears about yourself or your work. Then, write His response in your heart and His peace in your mind.

_____

_____

_____

_____

_____

_____

_____

_____

▶ ▶ ▶ **Day 6** ◀ ◀ ◀

And we know that all things work together for good to them that love God, to them who are the called according to his purpose.

(Romans 8:28, KJV)

Hey, you survived your first week at work! That's as exciting as getting the job in the first place because now you know you can do it! Even if your work is hard, you've learned something new each day!

However, if your job doesn't require much effort, it may be fattening! Work that's "a piece of cake" soon stuffs your face with boredom, which, like excessive poundage, can be difficult to hide. First, a little yawn slips out. Then you try to stay awake by reading the novel inside your on-the-job training manual. For exercise, your fingers do the walking as you speed-dial friend after friend after friend.

It may *seem* as though you have your work caught up with nothing to do, but there's always something job-related. For example, at the end of His six working-days God rested from work. Nobody said He was exhausted! He just took a break from creating. Then, shortly thereafter, He began His work of *re*-creating.

That's where you come into His job sites. That's where you can know—not wonder, *know*—that God's love for you and your love for Him lets Him do His regular, ongoing job, which is *to work all things for your good.*

14

Your job is part of God's good purpose for you. He knows what you need for a snug fit into His will. So, if your work is a piece of cake now, the main course might come later. If it's tough chewing, your job will be more appetizing as you sink your teeth into it—and as what you learn begins to sink in too!

Prayer: Lord, help! I can't see everything that goes into re-creating my skin and bones and blood or building up my body. But You can, so I know You see what's going into my career-building too. Thank You for providing what I need. Help me to trust You to work everything for my good in Jesus' name.

Journaling with God: Talk with God about anything that's been hard to swallow during your first week at work.

_____

_____

_____

_____

_____

_____

_____

_____

_____

_____

▶ ▶ ▶ **Day**

7

◀ ◀ ◀

He is the head of the body,
which is the church.
Everything comes from him.
He is the first one who was raised
from the dead.
So in all things
Jesus has first place.

(*Colossians 1:18, NCV*)

Unless you're positive Jesus took the day off from your church, that's the place to be on your day off! Not only will you find Him there, you'll have fellowship with other people who believe in His presence at church, home, school, and on the job too.

Since you're no longer a full-time student, friendships from church can help to fill a social void. Former classmates have scattered, and that may suit you fine! But it may also make you feel lonely—especially if you haven't yet discovered new friends at work.

If you just want to chat with people, though, you can do that at home on your own time! But, remember: your day of rest is on *God's* time! He gave you this day for a break in routine, so you can refresh your body, mind, and spirit.

God also gave you this day so you could give it back to Him. He won't *take* back what He's given! But He realizes that, without His good gifts, you don't have much to give Him anyway! So, He's given you this special time.

What does God want in return? Regular church attendance? Sure, but that doesn't mean just showing up and getting paid with a prayer and a hymn! Nor does it mean plugging your spiritual battery into a sermon that gives you a charge for the week! Attending church means attending to Christ. As head of the church body, He's worth far more than your precious time! He's *worth* your *worthship* of Him.

Prayer: Heavenly Father, thank You for Your ongoing gift of time to me. Thank You for my church. Help me to worship You in a manner worthy of Christ's name.

Journaling with God: List characteristics of God—Father, Son, and Holy Spirit—worth worshipping (a word that comes from *worthship*). Ask Him to help you recall times you've seen these worthy aspects of Him at work in your life.

_____

_____

_____

_____

_____

_____

_____

_____

_____

_____

Day 8

*Slaves, obey your masters
in all things.
Do not obey just
when they are watching you,
to gain their favor,
but serve them honestly,
because you respect the Lord.*

(Colossians 3:22, NCV)

"Hey! Who do these people at work think I am? Their slave?" Probably! Since the last one hired is usually the first one fired, new kids have their heads on the block should anyone get axed from the payroll!

Real slaves, of course, would not have such worries! If they'd lived to tell you about it, any white bondservant or black slave in this country would say the one thing they did *not* worry about was getting fired! Hebrew slaves also didn't worry about finding another job in Egypt, nor did they fret about job opportunities during their exile in Babylon.

So, here's a rather unusual thought for you to consider: Slavery has its privileges! In every country on earth, a slave can grumble, drag feet, and sit down on a job any time the master's back turns. Talk about job security! That can be so tempting that fearful folks of every ethnic group or race may prefer staying in such a position to keep from having to go through what you did to find a job!

If, however, you do not want to be anyone's slave, you can rise above your enslaving conditions, immediately! How? By doing your job honestly and well, even when no one peeks over your shoulder, and by knowing who's your real Boss. When others order you around or tell you what to do, you can continue to work, even when your manager's back turns.

The one true Master, whom you *freely and willingly* serve, always sees your work. And He will never turn His back on you.

Prayer: Dear Lord, forgive me for ever thinking no one was looking! You always see what I do. Thank You for never turning away from me. Help me not to turn my back on You or the service you've given me to do in Jesus' name.

Journaling with God: Ask God to give you His thoughts on how you can serve Him—of your own free will—in your work.

_____

_____

_____

_____

_____

_____

_____

_____

_____

Day 9

Masters, give unto your servants
that which is just and equal;
knowing that ye also
have a Master in heaven.

(Colossians 4:1, KJV)

So, have you seen anything at work that just isn't fair? Sooner or later, you will, especially if your supervisor does not know there's a Master in heaven!

Justice and equality in the workplace come as a direct result of accepting God's standard. Unfortunately, however, even Christian managers may forget. When that happens, the standard may have nothing to do with what's just or equitable for all but just what one person wants! And even that can change from one supervisor to another or from one manager's moment-to-moment mood swings.

The scales of justice do not swing wildly! To be stable and constant, equality must begin from one point of view that remains the same. Otherwise, what seems fair one day will fly off the scale the next!

For example, before yardsticks came into being, people measured a yard of cloth from (not by) their noses. With the center of their own faces as a starting point, they extended the fabric as far as their own hand or wrist could stretch. But, as you can guess, a problem arose as measurements varied from one person to another. This inconsistency made anyone with short arms consistently short-changed!

Today, varying standards—from person to person, race to race, sex to sex, or time to time—make any workplace unequal. So, the only way to steady the scales is to have one standard from which to measure—a single, fair, equal, and just godly standard! Without the Creator of Justice as the Divine Measuring Rod, the gauge will vary. Worse, it will be centered in each person who is doing the measuring instead of extending to *every* hand—directly from the face of God.

Prayer: Dear Unchanging God and Father of All, thank You for the equal system of justice that comes only from You. Please help my workplace be a fair place to work in Jesus' name.

Journaling with God: Talk with God about any unfair, unjust, or inequitable practices you've noticed at work. Briefly list these situations, praying for the persons involved.

_____

_____

_____

_____

_____

_____

_____

_____

*Conduct yourselves wisely
toward outsiders,
making the most of the time.*

(*Colossians 4:5, NRSV*)

"Say, who do you think you are, telling me what to do?"

"I'm not! I was just offering a little suggestion."

"Yeah? Well, when you know your own job a lot, maybe you can help with mine a little!"

People might not say that to your face, but they will behind your back—especially if you're in a management position or have taken over the family business. But, in this second week on the job, you're still in an outside lane! Other workers will want you to park your soapbox in the company garage or hang your theoretical keys to success on the ring outside the door. That's fine except, right now, you have a squeaky clean windshield for seeing well!

Since your view hasn't been marred by office politics, disillusionments over company practices, or small personal annoyances, you can clearly see the situation. You might even be able to tell where your workplace is headed. You may see something or someone going the wrong way, yet, if you confront this too soon, it could mean a head-on collision—or your job!

Instead of speeding onto a curb or someone's sidewalk, wait for a godly, timely moment to work gradually toward an inside lane. In the meantime, use the fresh view you now have to write down your ideas for improvement while they're still clearly visible. Pray about those ideas too.

Be aware, though, that your thoughts may change as your peripheral view increases. Until you can take in the scope of everyone's job at a glance, you might not know exactly what's needed. What seems obvious at first may not be the same view you'd have from another seat! So buckle up to your own work, and let your driving force for change remain seated in God.

Prayer: Heavenly Father, I know that Only You have a perfect, unobstructed, 360-degree view, but I don't like some things I see at work. Thank You for showing me the right time or place for changes. Keep me well inside Your will in Jesus' name.

Journaling with God: Ask God to give you His view of what's going on at work. Note His thoughts in the space below, using this list as a reminder to pray for your workplace.

_____

_____

_____

_____

_____

_____

_____

Day 11

*Let your speech always be gracious,
seasoned with salt,
so that you may know
how you ought
to answer everyone.*

(*Colossians 4:6, NRSV*)

Questions! Questions! When you interviewed for this job, you probably answered more questions than you like. Within the limit of federal regulations, employers may have asked about personal matters. Yet you understood they had to know certain things, such as physical considerations or use of prescribed drugs, to see if you could easily handle your work.

Now that's past, you may be the one full of questions: *Hey! Who needed to know all that stuff about my personal life? What difference is it to my employer what I do on my own time after work? When do I get paid? Where is this job going? Why did the company need to know about that? How can I get some answers?*

Your questions may already be answered in the company manual, job contract, brochure, or other papers you got when you were hired. So read those carefully to see if you find the information you need. If not, ask seasoned employees. But keep in mind that, like salt, a sprinkle of questions and answers can go a long way! Too much at once may preserve an unpleasant moment forever! Too little may not give you a real taste of what you wanted to know.

On food, conversation, opinions, and question-and-answer sessions, salt brings flavor. On a fresh wound, salt stings yet helps to cleanse and heal. In large quantities, it cures, preserves, or prevents spoilage.

There's no real substitute for using salt, tastefully and gracefully, in speech! So, dash off your well-seasoned questions and answers when others at work can hear you and respond. Keep each conversation salted (never sugar-coated) with truth.

Prayer: Dear God, please help me know how to answer and how to question in season. Give me Your word of truth to speak in Jesus' name.

Journaling with God: List questions you have about your job, workplace, or conditions of employment. Discuss each with God, and listen for His answers.

_____

_____

_____

_____

_____

_____

_____

_____

▶ ▶ ▶ Day 12 ◀ ◀ ◀

Withhold not good from them
to whom it is due,
when it is in the power
of thine hand to do it.

(Proverbs 3:27, KJV)

"Hey! This can't be right! My paycheck should have been more than this! Who told that FICA guy to take all my money?"

After waiting two whole weeks (sometimes a month) to get your first paycheck, that moment can come as a big shock! Instead of getting paid, you may feel you've been charged with too many expenses!

Unless you work in the accounting department, you might not have realized so many deductions would be taken from your salary. But guess what? They have. So, as soon as you've stopped the tears, check your pay voucher to see what's been withheld.

Most likely, your withholdings include monies set aside for federal and (in most places) state income taxes, Social Security, and Medicare. So on April 15 you won't have to worry about income taxes since you've faced tax withholdings in smaller amounts throughout the year.

Do not think, though, that Medicare means you're paying for someone else's bill! You're not! The current occupants of that program are the same people who paid a high price for the freedoms you enjoy, including the freedom to be

employed. So, now that you're the one with a job to do, give what's due without withholding any gladness!

Rejoice in the power of the Lord! Rejoice in the freedom to come and go to work as you please! Rejoice, Lord willing, in the long unbroken process of getting paid!

Prayer: Dear God, I'm glad to get paid at last! Help me to receive Your good gifts, joyfully, with thanksgiving for this country and all persons who paid in advance for my freedoms and job. Help me to serve them and You well in Christ's name.

Journaling with God: Even if it's taxing, thank God for your country, job, salary, and people or things for which you're grateful. Withhold not your gratitude or this space from Him!

_____

_____

_____

_____

_____

_____

_____

_____

_____

► ► ► **Day 13** ◄ ◄ ◄

*For the Lord God
is a sun and shield:
the Lord will give grace and glory:
no good thing will he withhold
from them that walk uprightly.*

(Psalm 84:11, KJV)

You usually say a blessing—grace—at each meal, right? Well, you might want to say grace, regularly, over your meal-ticket!

The blessing of grace means *favor.* For example, if you are in someone's good graces, that person *favors* you. If you grace a dinner table with prayer, the meal sits on your tummy as agreeably as your *favorite* food—even if the actual menu is greasy, soggy, tough, undercooked, over-fried, or onionized liver!

At the moment, you may feel somewhat uneasy, seeing all of the deductions you agreed to handle before you knew what you were biting into. Those bites may include options, such as a credit union savings plan, health insurance, life insurance, or a stock purchase program.

With that menu, however, you do get dessert! Although it may seem as if you're paying plenty, the price goes up for individual servings. For instance, if you bought insurance on your own, you'd pay more than group rates cost. You'd also have to remember to keep up payments, take time to write and log the check in your checkbook, get and address an envelope, go to the post office, buy postage,

and mail the payment before your insurance exits a grace period not known for its good graces!

So, as you reconsider your options, think about this: Income may come and go, but the hand of God withholds nothing good or glorious from those who stand upright before Him. Unless you choose to withhold your sins, you can personally deduct them in the power of God's forgiveness! Immediately, you can receive His blessing, be graced by His favor, and be acceptable through His Son who secured your debt on a cross. It's your option—paid in advance by your company in Christ.

Prayer: Heavenly Father, praise You for taking care of debts I didn't know I had and for gracing me with the name and company of Jesus.

Journaling with God: Talk with God about staying in His good grace through regular confession and belief in His Son.

_____

_____

_____

_____

_____

_____

_____

The people asked Jesus,
"What are the things God
wants us to do?"
Jesus answered,
"The work God wants you to do
is this: Believe the One he sent."

(John 6:28–29, NCV)

Okay, so maybe you need to work on Sunday after all! On your day off (and throughout the rest of the week) your main job is this: Believe that Jesus is the Christ, the Messiah, the Savior, the Anointed One sent by the Loving God.

Sometimes, it really is work to believe in Christ! When you're tired, disappointed, angry, worried, inconvenienced, ill, or otherwise miserable, you do hard labor to believe! Trusting in God's goodness and the saving power of His Son may take more effort than leaping cliffs! Who knows what will happen? God does, but He may let you go far beyond your limits!

Why? Why would a loving God let you run into hardships, hurt, rejection, mistreatment, or other hazardous situations? Often, upsets come from setting hope on your own abilities or someone else's instead of placing faith on the Rock. Maybe you jumped off because you felt like it. Maybe you slowly skidded or accidentally tripped. Maybe somebody pushed you. But, regardless of the situation or its causes, God can use an upset to set things upright again.

If uninvited, though, God may back off and let things slide, upside down, until you're ready to return—right side up—to Him. He won't work against you, but sin in yourself, other people, or the world will work hard to make you tumble!

As long as sin exists, you can be wrongly turned. But as you trust daily in the One God sent, your work of faith stabilizes in His work—the business of overcoming all that sin working around you and working around the clock too! A leap of belief in God may work you overtime, but any day of the week, your faith becomes a job well-done!

Prayer: Heavenly Father, help me to go to sleep each night and awaken each morning with thoughts of Your love working for me. Help me to begin every day by leaping out of bed and into my faith in the saving power of Jesus' name.

Journaling with God: Talk with God about anything that's made you slack off working your faith in Him.

_____

_____

_____

_____

_____

_____

_____

_____

_____

► ► ► Day 15 ◄ ◄ ◄

*I will set no wicked thing
before mine eyes:
I hate the work of them
that turn aside;
it shall not cleave to me.*

(Psalm 101:3, KJV)

You believe in God and His goodness, right? Well, do you also believe in evil and its badness? One without the other doesn't have much of a job to do with you!

A quick look around you shows all sorts of evil at work in the world. In your job, you may have already glimpsed bad tempers, a perverted system of justice, or wrongdoings that range from padding customer accounts to pilfering postage to making personal long distance calls on the company phone. You may have noticed job injuries, faulty equipment, unfavorable working conditions, or objectionable business practices. You may have felt ill will from ailing attitudes, disharmony, disorder. So? Is this news?

Ever since some kid shoved you in kindergarten, you've known that people can hurt each other, right? Nothing has changed. People either grow up and beyond uncivil behavior, or they grow a whole lot better at acting badly!

You have two options: Go with the action, or propel changes as God guides. Being idle or impartial sounds like a tempting gear. But, just as a neutral vehicle can easily be pushed up a hill or downhill, so can you—even if you don't see what's coming! Since you do see, though, you're

caught in a forward motion *or* a reversal of the current trend.

But here comes the hard part! Seeing what needs to be changed, you fix your eyes on the One from whom all good changes come. Don't set wickedness before your eyes or carry it home with you from work! Look to God to show you how to steer your workplace away from anything that's not right. Look to Him to give you an eye toward what is good.

Prayer: Heavenly all-seeing God, I praise You for Your pure and holy view. You alone know what's best at work. Help me to see what You see and do what You'd have me do in Jesus' name.

Journaling with God: Note specific changes you believe are needed in your workplace. Then ask God to bring to your mind His view on each matter.

_____

_____

_____

_____

_____

_____

_____

_____

_____

▶ ▶ ▶ **Day 16** ◀ ◀ ◀

You hypocrite!
First, take the wood out
of your own eye.
Then you will see clearly
to take the dust
out of your friend's eye.

(Matthew 7:5, NCV)

Have you noticed how vague criticisms and generalized complaints don't do much good at work or anywhere? Like big clouds of dust on a dry, windy day, they stir everything up and then settle in thin layers, making skin itch and eyes water! If you wait long enough, bad atmospheric conditions in your workplace might blow over. Meanwhile, you can sneeze, complain about complaints, stir things up to cloud the issue, look elsewhere for a perfectly pollution-free job environment (yeah, right) or take a dose of truth like an antihistamine.

Under emotionally-stirring conditions, true and specific facts clear the air. For example, your workplace may be obviously understaffed. You know because you hear employees gripe about it all the time! But these overworking conditions don't help you learn your job better. Every time you ask a simple question, someone answers, "Don't bother me, kid! Can't you see I'm busy?"

After a couple weeks of this, you feel like yelling, "Would someone just answer me?" Or you ask quietly, "Would somebody please explain this to me?" Or you've had it up to here and want to scream, "Would everybody stop telling me what to do!" Well, *would* they?

You get the drift. But, as soon as it settles, remove every "would," and then you will see clearly what's bothering you! You'll be able to address real concerns: "I know we're understaffed, but I can help if I have specific instructions *before* I try to do my job." Or, "I appreciate the help, but I have more information than I can absorb. Could we write this down for me to refer to when I reach that point in my work?"

Bits of truth in a cloud of innuendo only make facts hard to see. But, as you identify a true problem, you'll be able to focus on a solution and clearly know what to do.

Prayer: Dear God, worrying about all the *would-be* problems is clouding my view! Please help me to see the real issues at work in myself and on the job in Jesus' name.

Journaling with God: Have you wished everyone or everything at work would change but you? Discuss your job climate with God, and listen prayerfully to His response.

_____

_____

_____

_____

_____

_____

*One who is slack in his work is
brother to one who destroys.*

(*Proverbs 18:9, NIV*)

In many business places, Monday gets off to a slow start.
Then the work winds down again before the weekend. So,
instead of a five- or six-day work-week, some employees
act as if a full-time job means maximum acceleration every
Wednesday!

A steady pace each day helps to get the job done. If you
happen to work in a busy place that's also understaffed,
your pace may be somewhat higher than the norm. If you
landed a job requiring little effort, your pace may be slightly
above a snoozing zone!

Fast or slow, cruising at a constant speed throughout the
week keeps you from slacking off work. Every day, you'll
progress toward completing your list of "things to do" for
that day. Then, at the end of the week, you won't need to
rush into overtime nor slack off early and let work slide into
a downhill heap of trouble!

Since your work is yours to do, ignoring it won't make it
go away but merely delays it until Wednesday—or Thurs-
day. But while it waits, idle work won't sit idly. It slides. It
mounts. It builds at an alarming, break-neck speed, then,
crash! It destroys present progress, annihilates future
chances for promotion, demolishes the work area, slaugh-

ters self-image, eradicates sweet dreams, and exterminates peace of mind on the one day of the week that's meant to be restful!

Slacking off opposes effort and destroys the work force. Too little too late not only won't get the job done, it may also end a position altogether! But, if you find a workable pace for doing today's work while it's still today, the only thing you'll need to do tomorrow is *one* day's job, which is plenty! You won't slack off. You'll just stop work, go home, and rest—letting the rest of the week bide its time.

Prayer: Dear Father, help me begin each workday with thoughts of You and what You'd have me do this day in Jesus' name.

Journaling with God: Do you have too much or too little work to do? Discuss this with God, asking Him to give you ideas for fitting specific tasks to each day of the week.

_____

_____

_____

_____

_____

_____

_____

_____

Day 18

Does your workplace seem like a circus? "Hurry! Hurry! Right this way! See the amazing new employee juggle twenty tasks! See the giant workload disappear before your very eyes! See an incredible crew cut through mounds of paperwork. See the assembly line stay in step with the precision of a yes-we-can-can dance. See the company dynamo shoot into the next round of promotions. See tightrope workers balance on a down-to-the-wire deadline."

Whew! Watching such a show can be a fanfare or a nightmare! But, as part of the program, you get your act together for a paid performance daily! Your routine takes rehearsals with no unnecessary delay.

Often, though, people postpone action, not from laziness or lack of interest but from lack of organizational skill. In the beginning, a new job can be overwhelming. Yet work eases through diligent planning for each new feat.

For a successful work performance, first note specific duties—nothing more and nothing less than the tasks you've been assigned. Plan your routine by listing what's needed for that particular day, and schedule all aspects of the performance. For instance, if your job includes making coffee, the steps involve scouring the pot, replacing the filter, filling the grinds, and adding water. If you're in management, you get to pick out the coffee and buy it too!

You do not, however, have to juggle hot cups or squirt cream into someone else's mug! You don't have to cater or hurry, hurry, hurry! But, as you move steadily toward a well-balanced job performance, your work profits the whole company. You just do your job—without any need for barkers, fanfare, or amazing feats of speed.

Prayer: Lord, help me to plan each day's work and carry out each task, diligently and well in Jesus' name.

Journaling with God: Make a list of the specific tasks your job requires. Ask God to help you see the individual steps involved in planning and performing your work.

_____

_____

_____

_____

_____

_____

_____

_____

Day 19

So, how ambitious are you? Here's a pop quiz! (And you thought you'd finished tests forever.)

1. Do you (A) aim to please anyone and everyone at work or (B) just get your job done?

2. Do you (A) aim to uncover in-house affairs or (B) mind your own business?

3. Do you (A) aim to be distracted by every single thing you dislike or (B) lead a quiet job life?

4. Do you (A) aim to do what you want or (B) do as instructed?

5. Do you (A) aim to meddle, fiddle, doodle, and dabble or (B) work with your hands and other parts (muscle, brain) needed for your job?

You've probably guessed that (B) answers help you BElong at work and, hopefully, BE long employed! But these busy (B) answers also help you BEaware of what needs doing, BElieve in your performance, BEhave properly in your job, and steadily BEcome more proficient.

Consider, though, the opposite ways to BE at work: BEwildered by what's going on, BElittling yourself or other employees, BEside yourself with worry, BEtraying confi-

dences, BEtween jobs, BEreft of income, or just plain BElly-aching all the time!

Since you face those daily options to BE, your choices will help you aim toward your ambitions. Your decisions will point you in a particular direction. So your very BEst choice is, first, to know God's ambition for you. Then aim to oBEy! An ambition aimed toward oBEdience to God will eventually bring you a peaceable, productive, satisfying, and hopefully, very long job life!

Prayer: Heavenly Father, please help me to aim for poise in my position so I can do my work well, handle problems without getting ruffled, and mind my own busy-ness in Jesus' name.

Journaling with God: Ask God to show you any aims at work that need to be reconsidered or redirected.

Each one should test his own actions.
Then he can take pride in himself,
without comparing himself
to somebody else.

(*Galatians 6:4, NIV*)

First the bad pride: "I'm the greatest! Nobody can do this job as well as I can! This company should be grateful to have me for an employee! I'm faster, smarter, stronger, and better than anyone!"

Now the good pride: "I'm glad this job is going well. I'm grateful to have honorable work with a reputable company. I feel good about my overall job performance. I'm so much faster, smarter, stronger, and better than I was when I first began to work here."

Those differences probably aren't bad or good news to you, but both attitudes carry bold headlines! Some people head to work each day with pride, thinking well of themselves and the job they're doing. Others have it in their heads that they're better than anyone else, or they think the sky has no limit while their current jobs are ten miles below!

Being proud isn't the same as taking pride in a job well done. If you're not sure about that, test your actions. Have you compared your mentality or muscles to others at work? Have you felt miffed or murderous when another employee received a prize you thought you deserved? Do you covet someone else's job so badly you've already begun a game of musical chairs to change positions? Do you have your head in the clouds, thinking you rate with archangels?

A proud attitude compares self to others, looking up to or down on them. But taking pride in one's work stays lateral—looking straight ahead and comparing self to self. By refusing to compare yourself to anyone, you can take pride in your accomplishments and progress, knowing that your job and your very self are incomparable gifts straight from God.

Prayer: Heavenly Father, help me to look down on no one and look up to You alone. Help me to feel good about myself and take pride in my work in Christ's name.

Journaling with God: Most Christians have some area in which they feel a bit smug or proud of themselves. Ask God to show you any pride you have, discussing it with Him in this space.

_____

_____

_____

_____

_____

_____

_____

Day 21

*Unfriendly people are selfish
and hate all good sense.*

(*Proverbs 18:1, NCV*)

◀ ◀ ◀

Guess what? Everyone at work doesn't aim to please God. That's no big surprise, but other people's ambitions might stun you like a poisoned dart! As aspiring employees aim toward what they want, anyone or anything that's in the way can become a potential game trophy!

Since you've recently entered the work world, your new position may be below other peoples' sites. But, if any employees around you aim for another job, they might think you're after theirs! No matter how pleasant you are, they may treat you unkindly or act downright unfriendly!

Shooting big or small game can become a nonsporting event in any workplace. Sometimes, people know exactly what they want and go after it without caring who's affected or afflicted! Others just aim to get ahead, shooting down people without really meaning to hurt anyone. Still others, with no particular aims or goals, may senselessly shoot off their mouths, sending poisonous arrows darting in every direction!

If you're in the middle of such unhappy hunting grounds, you might feel like running for cover! You might want to camouflage your true self so no one notices you. You might even find yourself considering how to set up an ambush to snare a coveted position you'd like to have. But, rather than covering up these aims, head toward open ground!

Set your sights on serving God, and you won't get caught in an underbrush of senseless, selfish pursuits! By making it your ambition to please Him, you'll have the good sense to drop your ammunition and extend an open hand of friendship to everyone at work. You'll have nothing to hide, so others will eventually see you're not out to snag them or their jobs!

Prayer: Dear Father, help me aim to please You in all that I do at work in Christ's name.

Journaling with God: In your journaling space, pray for those who seem hostile toward you or other employees.

_____

_____

_____

_____

_____

_____

_____

_____

_____

► ► ► **Day 22** ◄ ◄ ◄

Reckless words pierce like a sword,
but the tongue
of the wise brings healing.

(Proverbs 12:18, NIV)

Has anyone at work tried to attack you with words like, "Are you stupid or what?" Has someone pricked you with disgruntled remarks about your ability, position, or salary? "You must think you're pretty smart, earning as much as it's taken me ten years to get!"

Older dissatisfied employees may occasionally criticize out of habit, but, if you're pierced by their comments, you may need to put a stop to such remarks. One way may be to find their weak spots and criticize them! But that would be unkind—and unwise. Dueling in daily word matches won't help either.

Offensive matches bring casualties. In-house combats cause uncivil war. Clashing personalities, battling wits, contending dispositions, and other fighting matters devastate the workplace and take employees hostage.

Consider, though, God's alternative: *A word of wisdom brings healing.* This means you do not wound an offender by recklessly saying whatever hurls from your mouth! But neither do you stand around like an immobilized target while other employees take their best shot at you!

You can take aim with prayer by asking God to give you His healing word for a particular person or situation. He will! You know this because God gives whatever you need to obey Him. Also, you never know what healing word will tend someone else's old injury, but God knows! Trust Him each day to go to battle for you—not hatefully but lovingly—with the power of His wisdom at work to heal.

Prayer: Heavenly Father, I know that words can kill or heal. Thank You for giving me Your Word in Jesus' name.

Journaling with God: Talk with God about killing words that cause pain. Ask Him for His healing word about each person or situation at work that troubles you.

_____

_____

_____

_____

_____

_____

_____

_____

_____

Day 23

A soft answer turneth away wrath: but grievous words stir up anger.

(Proverbs 15:1, KJV)

Good grief! You probably haven't been on your job long enough to accumulate too many grievances, but other employees have! Perhaps they expected to get a promotion, a raise, a day off, or a work bay with windows. Yet, when time came for them to collect, the person in charge may have forgotten that they—or all the big promises—even existed.

Instead of speaking to the boss about unfair situations, older employees may take their grievances to the newest, most uninvolved person around—which happens to be you! Some will fire off a long list of complaints or explode against company policies in general. Listening to such heated remarks can be enough to singe anyone, but if you're engulfed by the flames, you just might feel torched off!

In potentially blistering situations, a soft answer not only turns away the other person's wrath but yours too. It's unlikely you'll get "hot under the collar" if you keep a cool head, right? Well, by remaining in a coolly objective position, you also help to lower emotionally-charged reactions and stop tempers from flaring around you.

Keeping your cool doesn't mean you'll be disinterested or apathetic. You just won't strike matches that broil you or fuel someone else's flame. You won't scorch anyone with a blast of heated words. You will bring a calming view and soft glow of friendship to each situation that arises.

Soft answers seldom get anyone fired up or fired! With God's help, you can prevent igniting still another grievance.

Prayer: Dear God, people at work seem highly combustible about some topics! Please give me a soft answer that neither dampens spirits nor inflames. Thank You for keeping Your Holy Spirit kindled within me in Christ's name.

Journaling with God: Discuss with God any heated situation in your workplace, including the smoke screens people may use to cover hard feelings.

_____

_____

_____

_____

_____

_____

_____

_____

_____

_____

▶ ▶ ▶ **Day 24** ◀ ◀ ◀

He healeth the broken in heart,
and bindeth up their wounds.

(Psalm 147:3, KJV)

So, how's the job going? Is it okay, all right, great, terrific, terribly disappointing, or just so-so?

When you took this job, you may have started with your chin up, determined to make the best of a low-entry position. You might have been pleased to have any job and excited about your future prospects. Most likely, you felt glad to be able to earn a regular income even if that meant getting paid less than you wanted. You knew you had to begin somewhere, and you figured this was as good a place as any.

Now that the newness has worn off, you may be wondering if you made a mistake. Or if you felt heartbroken from the start in taking a job that didn't utilize your skills or training, you may be relieved now that the sharp pain has quietened to a dull ache. Perhaps you like your job just fine and are confident about your future, but now you're realizing that you have to show up for work every day, whether you want to or not! You can't just convince your parents you have a stomachache in order to skip school! Even if you stay home and snooze, your work doesn't stop.

No matter whether you enjoy your job a little or a lot, everything isn't perfect! Some aspects of your work are uncomfortable. Others are hard to accept, and adjustments have to be made. That's normal—and so is the stress that comes from the changes you're experiencing.

The heartache every adult faces is this: You're grown up now. You're earning your own way. Yet you cannot help but grieve an important loss you may not have really considered—the loss of your childhood. As you let go of those days, look to God for healing—for healthy new growth and a speedy recovery of joy! Despite your job or age, you can take heart in knowing you will always be God's cherished child.

Prayer: Heavenly Father, I praise You for being my Perfect Parent. Childhood days weren't always happy or fun, but they seem more so now that they're past. Please heal any lingering hurts I have, and bind any wounds I've childishly caused others. Thank You for helping me fully recover in Christ's name.

Journaling with God: Reminisce with God about the childhood days still affecting you, and seek His healing as needed.

_____

_____

_____

_____

_____

_____

*Whoever ignores the poor
when they cry for help
will also cry for help
and not be answered.*

(*Proverbs 21:13, NCV*)

"Hey! What's going on around here?"

One of the innocences of childhood comes from not even knowing that *anything* is going on! Young children seem to relate events to themselves, so they seldom feel other people's pain.

By high school or college, you may have begun to feel the pain of others deeply. But, since you weren't able to do much about it, you may have externalized the discomfort by telling yourself things such as, "I don't feel sorry for those people! They brought this on themselves." Or "They could change their condition if they really, really wanted to."

Some adults still think that way! Maybe you've run into them at work. They seem to goad people unlike themselves into becoming whatever they are! They look down on differences, especially those of another race, sex, lifestyle, or belief. They turn a deaf ear to any grievance, complaint, or cry, childishly thinking it has nothing at all to do with them.

Hopefully, this isn't going on in your workplace. But, if it is, you may feel like a child who's been rudely yanked from a nap! You might feel dazed or fuzzy-headed about the real issues or afraid of getting involved. You may wish you could go back to sleep as if nothing unpleasant occurs in your dream job. You may feel caught in someone else's nightmare.

Before you get involved in any conflict, however, ask God to give you a winsome way of speaking. If necessary, be willing to wait until your own good work gives you a stronger voice in your workplace. Then, be ready to act—in a highly informed and loving manner—to do what you can to help those who just aren't being heard.

Prayer: Dear God, I don't want to shut my ears to anyone's cry if there's something I can do. But I do not like to hear about misery when I can't do anything about it! Thank You for always being able to help. Please remind me to speak to You about everything I hear, knowing that You Alone have the power to help, heal, and save in Jesus' name.

Journaling with God: Talk with God about conditions—at work or in your community—that concern you.

_____

_____

_____

_____

_____

_____

_____

▶ ▶ ▶ Day 26 ◀ ◀ ◀

*Those who ignore instruction
despise themselves,
but those who heed admonition
gain understanding.*

(*Proverbs 15:32, NRSV*)

It's bad enough that you can't ignore other people's problems! You can't even ignore your own! Like growling tummies, they won't settle down. Just when you thought you'd finished selecting courses at school, you've begun to see you'll always have something new to learn. That's true. You will. But to *digest* what you learn, you need an appetite for truth. You need to swallow correction—willingly—whether you're seventeen, twenty-one, fifty-five, or ninety-nine!

Right now though you have another problem. You're still in a thirty to ninety-day probation period at work, which means that—without any warning—you can suddenly find yourself in an unemployment line! Since you've obviously chosen working over waiting in line to be fed, you can see it's to your advantage to keep moving toward a better understanding of your job.

But there's another problem! Your supervisor may not be giving you the information that would help you do your job well. Yet that very same person may quickly reprove your slightest blunder!

Even after you've been on the job a while, you may have to accept correction in order to learn, but that's palatable if you hunger to know what's true. By *wanting* to understand—as much as you want to eat each day—you'll be able to take the correction you need. You'll accept admonition as a wedge of truth that nurtures your understanding, and you'll know it's being delivered, right on time, by the Lord.

Prayer: Dear God, thank You for providing for my ongoing education. Help me to remain teachable in Your Holy Spirit in Christ's name.

Journaling with God: Do you find it difficult—at work or elsewhere—to accept correction? Talk about this with God.

_____

_____

_____

_____

_____

_____

_____

_____

_____

_____

▶ ▶ ▶ **Day 27** ◀ ◀ ◀

*Have nothing to do
with the fruitless deeds of darkness,
but rather expose them.*

(*Ephesians 5:11, NIV*)

Aren't you glad that correcting other people isn't your job? Okay, so maybe it is!

If you've begun a management position or a career in teaching, you've already discovered that your job description includes discipline. Not only do you discipline yourself, you police the behavior of other people too. Or maybe you're on patrol for your city, county, state, or nation and understand the need to correct any transgressions against society.

But what if you're a store clerk who sees an employee dipping into a cash drawer? What if you happen to spot a genteel, elderly lady bagging breath mints? What if you catch a cute little kid swiping a roll of toilet paper? What if you see a big bad-looking dude pocketing a pocket New Testament with Psalms? Are you going to say anything?

Maybe it's worse! Maybe you overheard an employee on a company phone talking a few times to a friend in Taiwan. Maybe you saw people clocking overtime in the employee's lounge while they labored over television reruns.

Maybe you heard a dramatic but damaging rumor that you know just isn't true. Are you going to do anything?

No job description includes policing the whole world—just the one around you. Unless you're in politics, it's not your job to make new laws or set standards to suit yourself. You can't go by what's popular—or even what *seems* to be compassionate. You go by what God says. So if you see people breaking commandments against stealing, lying, cheating, or harming anyone, your company's business is your business too! Just be careful, and don't take part in wrongdoing by covering for someone else.

Prayer: Heavenly Father, You see everything that's going on and always know what to do, but I don't! Please give me Your wisdom and an understanding of Your will in Jesus' name.

Journaling with God: Ask God to bring to your mind specific actions He wants you to take regarding the actions of others.

_____

_____

_____

_____

_____

_____

_____

_____

Do you work with the public? If so, the Bible gives a clear, direct, and timely guideline for your job—like an inner-office memo from God, sent out this very morning!

God didn't need intercoms, air waves, or cables to tell you what you would encounter in dealing with people today! He knew! Customers or clients may contact you by mail, phone, fax, computer, or satellite dish, but from one age to the next God's instructions remain the same. And, His word is this: Don't show favoritism. Treat everyone just alike—just like you want to be treated.

You already know the Golden Rule, right? Well, all you do now is apply that to your job experiences. Consider these potential situations for example:

• A child comes to your check-out counter only moments before a well-dressed, middle-aged man wants your help. Who gets your attention first?

• A seedy-looking old woman drops into a booth and asks you for a glass of water. You're certain she won't tip for a free item, but she's taken your only free table at high noon! Do you refuse to serve her unless she buys something?

• A close friend or family member wants to buy an insurance policy from you, but the appointment happens to be on a particularly hectic day. Do you skip informative parts of your presentation since you're already sure of a sale?

So how does your work line up? Do you treat customers as you'd want to be treated if you were the child, the down-and-out person, the friend? Or do you show partiality toward people with a stronger voice, more money, and less tolerance of you personally? Are you partial only to pleasing God?

Prayer: Dear God, I didn't realize I'd practiced favoritism! Like angels, some types are hard to see! Help me always to be aware of what's fair and true in Jesus' name.

Journaling with God: Discuss with God any customer-related experiences you find confusing or hard to handle.

_____

_____

_____

_____

_____

_____

_____

_____

▶ ▶ ▶ **Day 29** ◀ ◀ ◀

Don't let anyone look down on you because you are young, but set an example for the believers in speech, in life, in love, in faith and in purity.

(1 Timothy 4:12, NIV)

Since you probably began this job on the ground floor, most positions in your workplace rank higher than yours. But that doesn't mean you have to walk around with the back of your head parallel to the floor! Even if you look up to some people, that doesn't mean they have to look down on you.

Okay, so you're less experienced than most employees! They know what they're doing in their jobs while you're not always sure in yours. They get to choose their paid vacation time while you only get certain days off and national holidays. You have fewer choices, fewer benefits, fewer rights, and a smaller voice at work. So?

Although you're still new in your job—and maybe even new to being an adult—you carry a lot of weight! To your workplace you bring freshness that can't be packaged. You bring new thoughts, new opinions, new creativity, and a new perspective. You are an original!

At times, people may expect too much from you, but they don't expect you to be an antique! There are plenty of older employees whose job experiences have made their mouths sag, their feet drag, their enthusiasm lag, their words nag, their fingers wag, their moods jag, and their honesty, modesty, faith, and purity zig—or zag, depending on how you look at it. So even though you don't have much job experience—or even many experiences as an adult—you do have you. You have what *only you* can bring to a situation. You have newness. You have God.

Prayer: Heavenly Father, thank You for the freshness of my working world and Your ongoing re-creation of me—most recently from child to adult. Help me to grow evenly in my faith and show myself always to be Your child in Jesus' name.

Journaling with God: Ask God how He would have you be an example of His Love at work.

_____

_____

_____

_____

_____

_____

_____

_____

_____

_____

Day 30

But one is tempted by one's own desire, being lured and enticed by it.

(James 1:14, NRSV)

Isn't temptation great! Without it, you'd be tempted to think you're perfect, and therefore not in need of God! You'd have trouble spotting weaknesses—which often show up during temptation or times of testing. (Just don't confuse the two!)

Testing (of faith, character, love) may come from God—not to *weaken* but to *strengthen* what's tested. Although it may be unpleasant to take, a test examines your comprehension of spiritual matters and your personal application of what you've learned so far. When you see those test results, you then know what needs correcting or studying more. The purpose isn't to flunk you but to help you progress toward God.

Temptations have the opposite effect. They never come from God because, as the Bible clearly states, God tempts no one. His enemy does, though, and so you need to be aware of that source of allurement. The purpose of temptation is to steal, kill, or destroy what belongs to God (in this case, you!) by enticing you further and further away from Him.

Although testing and temptation have opposing goals, they play on a similar field! Almost any field of desire will do since your desires have the ability to bring you closer to God—or make you run in the opposite direction!

Sometimes, you don't know a desire even matters to you—until temptation helps you see. For instance, maybe you did not realize how much you want to please people until you kept trying to fit in with employees after hours at a bar. Or maybe you've been tempted to follow sexual desires toward someone's enticing advances. But instead of flopping into bars or beds, you realize what you *really* want is wholesome companionship and, perhaps someday, a Christian spouse. So, in prayer, you bring that highly desirable subject to God.

Prayer: Thank You, Lord, for leading me not into temptation but into knowing what entices me. Thank You for Your strength at work in me to follow Your ways in Jesus' name.

Journaling with God: Ask God to bring to your mind any fields of desire tempting you. Then, bring those desires to Him in prayer.

_____

_____

_____

_____

_____

_____

_____

"Honor your father and mother"—
which is the first commandment
with a promise—
"that it may go well with you
and that you may enjoy long life
on the earth"

(Ephesians 6:2–3, NIV)

Congratulations on completing your first month on the job! The work—and your adjustment to it—took patience, energy, and time. Each day you're learning more and earning more! So you probably don't want to be treated like a child.

If you're still living at home, you may be feeling as though nothing has changed since school days. Your old curfew keeps standing although you'd like to knock it down! You've brought this up but gotten nowhere, yet, when you try to slip in late and unnoticed, even the floorboards squeal on you! Your mom, dad, or sibling need rest, but you're just tired of a lack of privacy! Besides sharing a bed or bathroom, you have to share the television set, and during commercials anyway, the whole family seems set on watching you!

What's a working body to do? Regardless of the job age, you're to honor your father and mother, not because they say so but because the Bible does. In return, you'll have a much longer, better life—on the job and elsewhere too.

To honor means that you value what your parents say and hold their needs in esteem. You show consideration of them as individuals, not expecting them to carry you

64

around like an infant! If they can help you, they'll probably try because they love you. You will not outgrow that love. But demanding (or even just expecting) action, privileges, cash, time, or something else from them will dishonor them—and you.

Prayer: Dear God, thank You for always being my Heavenly Father. Help me to honor and obey You by honoring and obeying the parents and grandparents You've given me. Help me to see and value them as individuals—and as Your children too in the name of Your Son, Jesus.

Journaling with God: Talk with God about anything that's been troubling you at home, then offer each situation and person to Him in prayer.

_____

_____

_____

_____

_____

_____

_____

_____

_____

*All Scripture is given by God
and is useful for teaching,
for showing people
what is wrong in their lives,
for correcting faults,
and for teaching how to live right.*

(2 Timothy 3:16, NCV)

Have you been thinking about getting your own apartment? Have you charted a course in that direction, dropped anchor at home port (for now anyway)—or just been making waves? Worry keeps you snugly moored with only the freedom to bob around, depending on the current flow of cash or fears you harbor. Making waves sets you adrift from your family even though you're still anchored to them— which gets you nowhere! But planning steers you toward the next destination.

For example, you may want to be on your own but aren't yet ready. You can begin to navigate toward your workplace, making decisions about what living quarters you prefer, how much you can afford, whether you'll need a roommate to help with costs, and how much cash you can comfortably stow away before departure. Such plans head toward a favored route and sensible schedule before you ever leave the dock!

You don't, of course, know which way the wind will blow at home or work after you set sail. You don't know how well you've secured your job or what squalls you'll encounter. But you do know more about "sailing toward new horizons" than you may think! Wherever you go, God's Word goes with you.

Just as a sailor needs a compass or the north star to navigate, so do you need the Bible to steer you in the right direction. As you head into unknown waters, trust God's unfailing Word to guide you. By reading the Bible—over and over, cover to cover—you'll know how to get from here to there in all sorts of weather. Then, as you encounter a new situation or adverse condition, simply use a concordance to look up the topic of concern *before* you redirect your course.

Prayer: Heavenly Father, thank You for Your Word which guides me wherever I go. Help me to follow the sure course You set for me in Jesus' name.

Journaling with God: Discuss with God the worries you have about being on your own. Listen to His personal word to you which calms the sea of emotion or deluge of fear.

_____

_____

_____

_____

_____

_____

_____

_____

*And how from infancy you have
known the holy Scriptures,
which are able to make you wise
for salvation through faith
in Christ Jesus.*

(2 Timothy 3:15, NIV)

Do you ever wonder if you can take care of yourself? Most young people can't wait to be on their own. Yet if they're honest, they admit they're also scared. Some fear living alone or dealing with nosy landlords and ladies! Others worry about finding a roommate who can be trusted to leave a clean glass in the kitchen and food in the refrig and not make off with family heirlooms!

Despite your particular concerns, the real fear is this: *Do I have what it takes to be an adult?* The answer varies, of course, from one person to the next, but to you personally the answer is yes! You *do* have what it takes! Not only will you make it as an adult, you'll do just fine!

How can someone who doesn't even know you be so sure? The very fact that you've gone this far in your devotional time shows you not only have God in your life, you also care about what He wants. You've demonstrated at least an interest in Him, so you don't really need faith in yourself! You have chosen to place your faith in God.

Maybe you suspect that your faith is no bigger than a tomato seed, a blackberry seed, or a tiny little mustard seed. But you probably also realize that God is big enough to take something microscopic and make it grow. He's large enough to guide that growth, too, by providing what you need when you most need it. But even if He never gives you another thing as long as you live, God has already given everything that's necessary for you to make it as an adult! He's given you His Word to read and keep and follow. He's given you His Holy Spirit through Jesus Christ to grow you up in Him—and into eternal life.

Prayer: Dear Lord, You know how little faith I have at times, but, right now, it's all I've got. Thank You for accepting my gift, however small, and making it grow in Christ's name.

Journaling with God: Talk with God about your faith in the Lord Jesus Christ.

_____

_____

_____

_____

_____

_____

_____

_____

_____

*Using the Scriptures,
the person who serves God
will be capable,
having all that is needed
to do every good work.*

(2 Timothy 3:17, NCV)

Remember your first-day jitters when you first started your job? The first days of being on your own often bring more jitters than a jitterbug!

Maybe you don't believe in dancing! Maybe you fear you can't keep step with the typical tempo of adults. Maybe you'd rather go on side-stepping your family at home as long as possible or waltz through someone else's life and apartment and never have to find a pace, a place, or a song that suits you. Maybe you're just plain scared to take responsibility for the twists and turns of your own life. If so, you may feel better knowing that this, too, is pop music!

Most young people fear failure. They're afraid they'll trip up or step on someone else's feat! They know they can't rock back the clock into the fifties, yet they don't feel up to the current trend toward body slamming! You, however, do not have to play those same ole tunes. You can simply make a new selection—one that's right for you.

God's Word provides you with the words to the music He's personally set for you to follow. With Scripture and the Holy Spirit writing His lyrics within your heart, mind, and soul, you're equipped to do all that God asks. Not only can you take good care of yourself, you're now able to offer your services in helping other people too. Just do not let them guide you! At the very beginning of each new step, ask God to take the lead.

Prayer: Dear Heavenly Father, thank You for giving me courage and leading me skillfully as I practice steps in being adult. Help me to be sure-footed about where I'm to go and what I'm to do in Your perfect timing in Jesus' name.

Journaling with God: Ask God to take each fear you list below. Then listen for His word about the best timing for you to be out on your own.

_____

_____

_____

_____

_____

_____

_____

_____

_____

_____

*Morning by morning
they gathered it [manna],
as much as each needed.*

(*Exodus 16:21, NRSV*)

When you were little, did anyone try to coax you to eat something you didn't like? They may have said, "Think of the starving children!" You answered, "I'll share! Take anything green on my plate!" Now that you're planning your own bread and butter, you might wish you had some of those leftovers!

As you consider the expense of having your own place, do take food into account. Fast food consumes cash fast! A not-so-fast rule is: the more time a packaged meal saves you in the kitchen, the more hours it costs you at work! You won't be paying more for more quality or more quantity but for more of someone else's time in preparing less of a meal!

Frozen dinners, take-out, or fast foods usually contain fewer vitamins and minerals too. Check labels, and you'll see that some pre-packaged foods have just a bit more nutritional value than the boxes they come in! Worse, some strip natural nutrients and then replace them with unnatural counterparts.

A basic rule is this: The more natural a food is, the more likely it is to be wholesome for your health. Artificial sweeteners, chemically produced supplements, processed vitamins, or other counterfeits of nature just don't add up to a wholesome food budget!

So, get real! And don't wonder where you'll get your bread to butter. In sending manna from heaven, God supplied supernatural grain. The bread not only provided the needed, natural nourishment for His children, but every day for forty years the people had exactly the amount that each one wanted to eat. No one starved. No one fell ill. No one had to feast on anyone else's stale crust!

Prayer: Dear God, didn't lack of food make Your children go down to Egypt in the first place? I guess You showed them You can be trusted to provide! Please help me trust You too, knowing You'll always supply what's needed for my well-being when I turn to You in Jesus' name.

Journaling with God: Talk with God about the spiritual nourishment He's provided each time you turn to Him.

_____

_____

_____

_____

_____

_____

_____

_____

Day 36

Have you been thinking about where you live? Depending on your current conditions, you may be hoping you can move out soon, leaving behind your family's comfy home or a rented bunk in someone's basement.

You don't really want to move up—onto the top floor of a rickety building with seventeen flights of stairs. You'd much rather find a place with privacy and a view, central heat and air, gate guards in tiny brick houses, and maybe a pool where you can meet other individuals as you lounge around.

But you might not get what you want right this very second. You may have to wait a few months, years, or perhaps forever to have a place you've drooled over. The funny thing is that, unless you're trying hard to impress someone (whose true affections can't be bought anyway), all the fancies just won't matter—as long as you have a home.

If you're at the planning-a-move stage now (or plan to be there later), keep these thoughts in mind: You need a place to eat, sleep, hang out, and store essentials, such as food, clothes, and toothbrush—a reasonably safe place, not too far from work nor too near falling apart.

No matter how deluxe or how deprived your accommodations seem, remember too: This is not the real home. Your real home is in the Lord and in His Word. So, be at home with Him. Welcome Him. Sing of Him, and ask Him to stay.

Prayer: Dear Heavenly Father, thank You for giving me a place to live. I want You to stay with me always in Jesus' name.

Journaling with God: Is there something that keeps you from feeling at home with God? Talk with Him about this.

_____

_____

_____

_____

_____

_____

_____

_____

_____

_____

▶ ▶ ▶ Day 37 ◀ ◀ ◀

The rich rule over the poor, and the borrower is servant to the lender.

(*Proverbs 22:7, NIV*)

"Hey, I don't care about anything fancy! I just want my own place—and *soon!*"

That's great! Just be aware that now is the time you might be seeking the most comfortable possibilities. Unless your mind stays alert to ward off evils, it's easy to find yourself tempted by a desire for nice-comfy-cozy-comforts. "I can afford this place! Yeah, it's more than I meant to spend, but I've been needing to diet anyway."

Moving into a place on the proverbial shoestring allows no room for tying up loose ends! First and last, there's the rental and security deposits to make. Then comes a deposit on electricity, gas, telephone, and television.

If you have furniture, you'll have the cost of moving it. If you don't, you'll need to get some. And the next thing you know, you're browsing furniture galleries, exclaiming over leather loveseats that look lacquered in nail polish.

Where does it end? Don't even think about it! But, of course, you'll have to when those thick, windowed envelopes arrive from the credit card companies. Or when a friend or family member knocks on your solid-core, decoratively paneled wood door, reminding you that you owe plenty!

Instead of letting a desire for comfort enslave you at payback time, make the decision to start off on your own by paying as you go—*now* and not thirty days or one year later.

You may not like second-hand furniture and brown-paper-bagged windows, but you won't be paying and paying for something, long after the newness has worn off or the object has worn out! Besides, you'll be in debt to no one. And that's truly "being on your own" because, when you *owe* no one, no one but God *owns* you!

Prayer: Dear God, please help me just say no to temptations to spend and spend. I ask You to help me be sensible about each cent You've given me to use in Jesus' name.

Journaling with God: As you plan a budget that allows your basic needs to be met, ask God to bring to your mind His thoughts on your money matters.

_____

_____

_____

_____

_____

_____

_____

_____

_____

Day 38

Today the Lord has obtained your agreement: to be his treasured people.

(Deuteronomy 26:18, NRSV)

Ready to get your own place? Great! Now get ready to sign a lease. Putting yourself on a dotted line means you're responsible for proper use of property belonging to someone else, so do read what you're agreeing to—*before* you sign.

Most likely, conditions will include a certain amount of money payable on a certain date for a certain length of time—which obligates you to stay put awhile! If you're not sure you want to stick around too long, that's a disadvantage. But if you like the place well enough and can easily afford it, a lease also works in your favor.

The person from whom you rent must also commit to having you around at a set price for as many months as stated. This means the rent can't go up during that time. Nor can you be booted into the street on a dark and stormy night—assuming, of course, that you're paid up and haven't destroyed the whole place.

As long as you leave the lease and place standing, you have somewhere to call home. You may or may not be allowed to sublet to pets or partners nor let booze, babies, or boats permanently reside. Your home belongs to someone else, yet it's your own personal space for now.

In a way, you could say the same about your relationship with God. When you became a Christian, you signed the lease of a lifetime! You agreed to give up an old, temporary life for eternal being. You're still your own person—and perhaps on your own now too. But your body, mind and spirit house the very finest treasures—prized and precious property of God.

Prayer: Heavenly Father, help me to know the place You'd have me be—on my own, yet owned by You in Jesus' name.

Journaling with God: Talk with God about each place you're considering, and ask Him to show you His view from the top.

_____

_____

_____

_____

_____

_____

_____

_____

_____

_____

Day 39

*The Lord will make you the head,
and not the tail;
you shall be only at the top,
and not at the bottom—
if you obey the commandments
of the Lord your God.*

(*Deuteronomy 28:13, NRSV*)

Heads or tails? Do you know which affordable place you like the best? Will you settle on and into an apartment, condo, house, rented room, top floor, bargain basement with hot plate and cold water, or a flat-bottomed boat?

Flipping a coin won't help you decide! Besides, you probably know what you *want* to do anyway—you're just not sure if you *can*. There's that budget to consider and, most likely, the voices of family and friends, helpfully trying to advise: "Oh, you don't want to live in *that* neighborhood! Didn't you hear about all those break-ins?" Or "If you paint the walls neon green and add a dozen lights, perhaps it won't be quite so dreary." Or "Yes, it's fine, dear, but isn't it a bit small?"

If you're trying to please people, here's some truly helpful advice: Forget it! You can't. No one can—not even God Himself! (He did give people their own free will, right?) So folks will find *something* to gripe about, or else they'll envy what you have. Meanwhile, "keeping up with the Joneses" will water-log people with bills and make them have to float enough loans to sink Noah!

Your home is your ark and no one else's. It's your place. Maybe your only options right now seem like the bottom

dregs for rentals, but your choices won't stay there! They will move up, and so will you—not when others say so, but when God brings about the time. Meanwhile, you can *know* that you are *able* to do *anything* God says will keep you afloat—on top and not financially underwater.

Prayer: Dear God, please keep me from drowning in bills—and from rowing in circles! Thank You for rescuing me. Praise You for the Ark of Jesus' name.

Journaling with God: God knows what you need! Discuss your needs, and then listen. Let His thoughts drift into your mind and sink in, inflating your spirits and raising you to the top!

_____

_____

_____

_____

_____

_____

_____

_____

_____

_____

*Some of those present were saying
indignantly to one another,
"Why this waste of perfume?"*

(Mark 14:4, NIV)

Remember those people entertained by complaints? Well, if you have money pouring from your pockets, they'll complain about that too! They'll say something like, "I knew you were doing well in your job, but no one told me you could afford the Taj Mahal." Or "Why are you wasting so much money on such a big, fancy apartment?"

Most people don't mean to be unkind, but jealousy, envy, old grudges, comparisons, and pride make their company stink! A giving, forgiving spirit will perfume any place you are with sweet acceptance, love, and joy for you and your good fortune.

Decency has a scent. Its fragrance lingers long after a person leaves the room, and even the slightest whiff helps to bring that individual back in memory. But who wants to recall a foul odor? Who wants to remember the smell of stinginess?

If someone splatters unpleasantness against your place, let it not sink into your spirit. Be quick to rinse it off with your forgiveness. Splash yourself, that person, and your new home with prayer! Offer God the sweet, sweet smell of thanksgiving for all He's lavishly given you. Let an aroma of praise and blessing fill the air around you as you dwell in the generous, magnanimous, profuse, and pure-scented Holy Spirit of the Almighty God.

Prayer: Dear Holy God, I praise You for the sweet remembrance of Your presence in this place. Thank You for Your good gifts that overflow without a trace of stinginess. Thank You for pouring out Your love and forgiveness through the sacrifice of Your Son, Jesus Christ, and for anointing me—and now, my home—with Your Holy Spirit.

Journaling with God: Ask God to help you recall His sweetly generous gifts for your abundant life. Ask Him to fill you and your dwelling place with His Holy Spirit.

_____

_____

_____

_____

_____

_____

_____

_____

_____

Will anyone rob God?
Yet you are robbing me!
But you say,
"How are we robbing you?"
In your tithes and offerings!
(Malachi 3:8, NRSV)

A big concern you've had about finding your own place has probably been your safety. No one wants to decorate a thief's apartment or contribute to stolen merchandise sold by criminals.

If you've found a place with a security system, dead-bolts, or neighborhood watches, you've already located some effective "No Trespassing" signs. You can also give potential intruders reason to pause by leaving on a radio or light and having somebody pick up your newspaper or mail when you're away, so you won't go around announcing: No one's home! You can do what you can to avoid isolation and showiness too.

One of your primary security devices, however, is your God-given good judgment, which comes complete with uneasy feelings and internally flashing lights. So when alarm bells sound in your head or emotions, don't be too quick to turn them off before you've checked them out. They could be God's way of getting your attention to keep you from being robbed.

You can also ask what you can do to prevent the crime of robbing God! Most people with a Judeo-Christian background would be *amazed* to know they've taken what belongs to God—not by outright stealing but by withholding what's His as the giver of life, provisions, protection, and all good gifts.

You can't possibly repay God. But as you budget the cost of being on your own, give thought to how much He's given you. Then consider how much you can return—with praise—to Him.

Prayer: Heavenly Father, I haven't thought much about being accountable to You for my bank account! But, if I'm going to be on my own, I guess I can't expect my mom or dad or other Christians to give to You for me. Help me to know what You require of me in Jesus' name.

Journaling with God: Ask God to help you make out a workable budget that considers your needs—your number one need being Him!

_____

_____

_____

_____

_____

_____

_____

_____

▶ ▶ ▶ **Day 42**
◀ ◀ ◀

*"Bring to the storehouse a full tenth
of what you earn
so there will be food in my house.
Test me in this,"
says the Lord All-Powerful.
"I will open the windows of heaven
for you and pour out
all the blessings you need."*

(Malachi 3:10, NCV)

Sometimes Christians let their wallets off the hook by saying, "The New Testament doesn't say a word about tithing, so I don't have to!" They're right. It doesn't, and they don't! But now that you have a working concept of minimum wages and cost-of-living increases, you can see that, instead of cutbacks, Christians might do well to think about giving God a raise!

In Old Testament times, God asked His people to give to the Temple and those who ministered there. He wanted the priests, choral directors, musicians, and people providing janitorial or other services to receive the provisions they needed to stay alive and to keep on doing their duties. The people gave as though to God. In return, the ministers of the Temple gave the people leadership and a means of worship.

As a minimum guideline for giving, God set the tithe at 10 percent, with additional gifts above that as freewill offerings. Then, with the power of the Holy Spirit in the New Testament church, Christians gave all of their belongings to God! Instead of 10 percent, they gave 100 percent!

Anything less is God-way robbery! But, when you seek God first—giving all that you are and all that you own directly to Him—you put yourself in His protective custody and your cash in His safekeeping. If He promised to pour out blessings on those who gave a mere tenth of themselves, just think how much more He'll give to all of you!

Prayer: Dear Heavenly Father, help me to give myself to You without holding back. You know what I need better than I do, so I ask You to bring to my mind and heart the exact amount You want me to give to my church and other areas of Christian service—not just in money, but also in my time, talents, thoughts, and prayers in Jesus' name.

Journaling with God: If anything holds you back from offering yourself freely to God, talk with Him about this. Ask Him to let you know specifically what you're to give.

_____

_____

_____

_____

_____

_____

_____

_____

_____

> *They all ate and were satisfied,*
> *and the disciples picked up*
> *twelve basketfuls of broken pieces*
> *that were left over.*
> *(Matthew 14:20, NIV)*

◀ ◀ ◀

"Something's got to give!" That's how you may feel when you review your budget. Meals, housing, clothing, utilities, and reasonably reliable transportation to and from work can add up quickly—yet not add up at all! High costs and low wages might play tug-of-war anytime, but especially over your brand new wallet! Something has to give.

Way out in the wilderness—with no shelter, no change of clothing, no electricity, no vehicles, and no groceries in sight—Jesus told His disciples to feed thousands of people. The request just didn't add up! A few loaves of bread and even fewer fish could do nothing. Something had to give.

From the meager offering and the blessing of God through Christ, the Lord's disciples were—and still are— enabled to give and give and give. Everyone had more than enough—not because of their abilities but because of God's provision.

But that's not all of the story! The disciples, who had started out with very little food (certainly none to spare), had given all they had, probably thinking they'd go without a meal themselves. However, for their *five loaves* of bread, they got back *twelve baskets*, filled and overflowing. Not only did they eat well that day, they had food for other meals!

If you believe the Lord has asked you to give when you cannot easily afford it, just remember: When something's got to give, you can! By emptying yourself to God, you've freed your hold on things and worries—and opened your hands to receive basketloads of His good gifts delivered just for you.

Prayer: Dear Lord, I have so many expenses, I'm not sure how I'll take care of them myself. Help me to give by letting go of what I'm holding onto, whether it's worry or the money I meant to set aside for Your good purpose. Help me to receive all of Your provisions for taking care of me, in Jesus' name

Journaling with God: In every situation where you feel that something's got to give, give God your needs, worries, and fears, letting Him take good care of you.

_____

_____

_____

_____

_____

_____

_____

*Wise people's houses are full
of the best foods and olive oil,
but fools waste everything they have.*

(Proverbs 21:20, NCV)

As you make immediate plans or future preparations for being on your own, you're setting priorities. You're deciding what's important to you and rating your choices in numerical order. That's good planning—and smart!

Consider the alternative: Instead of deciding what's important and acting accordingly, you can dodge priorities by dealing with what comes up unexpectedly, or what demands your attention the loudest or longest! That, of course, would not be smart at all.

Sometimes, people avoid choices because they're afraid they'll make the wrong ones. What they don't realize is that making no choice *is* making a mistake—a big one! Without priorities, *everything* becomes top priority. So, people waste time, money, and effort by attending to things that don't matter while neglecting those that do. Eventually, the only success may be in wasting a whole life.

Your choices are not wasted! You're smart to have your kitchen stocked with wholesome food and your medicine chest with first aid supplies, such as rubbing alcohol and a box of sterile-wrapped bandages. Some items serve both purposes—honey (proven to be an effective antibiotic ointment for wounds), fresh garlic (shown to soothe stomachs,

ward off infections, and add zest to spaghetti), and olive oil (known to flavor salads and to coat dry pans or dry dish-pan hands too!)

So make a choice about being smart. Practice decision-making. Stock your shelves adequately. Then, be really wise about your choices by praying *before* you set your priorities.

Prayer: Dear Lord, please help me to get my priorities straight with You in Jesus' name.

Journaling with God: Make a list of everything you most need and want. Then ask God to arrange His order of preference.

_____

_____

_____

_____

_____

_____

_____

_____

_____

_____

*The sweet smell of perfume and oils
is pleasant, and so is good advice
from a friend.*

(Proverbs 27:9, NCV)

Does your income stretch to fit expenses? Most people have to skimp at first, and you might too as you make do with frayed towels or curtains. Second or third-hand furniture may be all that's available in a style you can afford. But there are things you can do.

On wooden floors, cabinets, and furniture, some elbow grease helps renew the sheen—and your spirits too. If no veneer covers the wood, you might also strip the old stain or varnish from a chest of drawers or table. Then restain, or leave the wood in a natural finish, coated with polyurethane.

For upholstery and drapes, you can usually freshen their appearance with special cleaners, spot removers, or plain ole soapy water. If ancient curtains won't survive a Laundromat, take them to a dry cleaner or shake and bake them in the sun. (When in doubt about the above, ask an experienced friend or family member for their home-refreshing advice.)

Scouring layers of dirt rids a place of musty smells and rejuvenates colors. If you only have a few dollars to invest in your decor, appropriate cleaning supplies might go at the top of your decorating list. With cash to spare, consider buying pillows in a favorite color found elsewhere in the room. By accenting what you like, you turn the mismatched furnishings into an eclectic look that's right for you. You also have comfy pillows to toss around or put behind your back that's aching from all this housework!

You'd probably prefer to decorate the place to suit you, and in time, you will. Meanwhile, gratitude for what you have works better than a room deodorizer, and the oil of gladness will make your place—and your face—shine!

Prayer: Dear God, thank You for my home! Help me to color it with Your presence and freshen it with Your Holy Spirit in Jesus' name.

Journaling with God: Make a list of everything you have to be grateful about. If you can't think of much, make a special point of offering God a *sacrifice* of praise!

_____

_____

_____

_____

_____

_____

_____

_____

Day 46

*The wise see danger ahead
and avoid it,
but fools keep going
and get into trouble.*

(Proverbs 22:3, NCV)

Being on your own doesn't mean you can't get help. It just means you can't *expect* any! Since you're not a child, you can no longer look to parents or other adults as backup. *You're* the adult now! But you're no fool!

Do you know what kind of person that is? Words like *dunce, dolt, blockhead* come to mind but don't say much about a fool's creation. *Foolishness, fooling around,* and *"I'm just foolin'"* give clues about typical foolish actions. But, to understand such a person (and, therefore, avoid *being* one) remember: Fools are those who fool themselves.

Frankly, at one time or another, everyone will act like a fool! You've seen it: A young man fools himself about his drinking, telling himself he's still in control. A boy fools himself into believing his friends won't like him if he's not tough. A girl fools herself about a boyfriend, sure that he will love her more if they have sex. A woman fools herself about her future, telling herself she'll never get ahead in her career. People fool themselves into believing God doesn't care what they do or what happens to them—that He isn't looking, or, worse, He isn't even around.

Only a fool pretends there is no danger. Only a fool has optimistic or pessimistic shields. But wise ones look ahead with realism—realistically facing the truth, identifying problems, finding solutions, and seeking help in Jesus' name.

Prayer: Dear God, I thought I could do this by myself, but I just can't! I thought that being cheerful and upbeat all the time would make everything okay, but it does not. I thought that nothing mattered, but it does. Please help me, Lord, to see things for what they are, realistically. Help me to look beyond my problems to the hope and help found in Your wisdom, in Your power, and in Jesus' holy name.

Journaling with God: If you have an uneasy feeling or a sense of danger, ask for God's help as you list specific concerns and offer them to Him in prayer.

_____

_____

_____

_____

_____

_____

_____

_____

_____

*Two people are better than one,
because they get more done
by working together.*

(*Ecclesiastes 4:9, NCV*)

If you have a super-big salad bowl, two heads of lettuce are better than one! A super-bowl-sized apartment may need a couple of heads together too.

By now, you have a pretty good idea of how much income you have and how much more you need. If you have a temporary or hardly noticeable gap between what comes in and goes out, you could take a second job to cover those expenses. But if you're stuck with an over-sized, financially inverted bowl on your head, consider having a roommate.

Two people can get more done together than they could alone—assuming, of course, that they work well as a team. Mathematically, doubling up will cover twice as much, but, if two people don't get along, whatever they have will soon be divided by the constant friction between them!

As you consider having a roommate to share expenses, don't toss together a once whole but now shredded friendship because it's what you have on hand! That would only top off the relationship with grated nerves! Just because you need more lettuce to make it on your own doesn't mean you have to settle for a roommate who's a cabbage head!

Be choosy about the basic ingredients you put into your home. Similar tastes or a colorful mix of personalities can work well together, especially if you're both well-seasoned Christians. So, if you feel that God wants you to select a roommate, carefully recall your friends, and find someone who's not quick to say, "I want" or "I demand," but "Let us . . . in Jesus' name."

Prayer: Heavenly Father, do I need a roommate? Please help me to consider options and know what You think. I need You!

Journaling with God: Weigh the pros and cons of sharing a place with another person, asking God to give you His view of each concern.

_____

_____

_____

_____

_____

_____

_____

_____

_____

_____

*Do not join those
who drink too much wine
or gorge themselves on meat.*

(Proverbs 23:20, NIV)

Did you hear the latest rumor? The one that used to go around said something about Christians being perfect. Now rumor has it that they can't be trusted about anything! You have seen the headlines: *Church Day Care Worker Charged with Molesting Child . . . Christian Parents Batter Baby . . . Minister Caught Ministering Drugs . . . Pastor Preys on Prostitutes.*

So, what do you think? Are Christians all good or all bad? Are they more righteous than other people, and if so, what difference does Christ make? Actually, Christians make the same mistakes as anyone.

Since they have God to guide, they might not make as many mistakes as often, but—like anyone else—Christians don't always want to hear what God has to say about their lives. Eventually, though, people who believe in the power of Jesus Christ will look to Him to be saved. They'll know and admit they've messed up and will seek God's forgiveness—not because of their own right standing with Him, but because of the righteousness of His Son, who was sent into the world to save sinners. In case you haven't heard, that's you!

That's also your potential roommate. You know because God's Word says *all* have sinned. What you can't be sure of, however, is whether another person realizes this yet. Even Christians make mistakes they're not yet ready to face: self-destructive, indulgent, or abusive choices about alcohol, drugs, food binges, sexual binges, or chronically bad attitudes.

God knows what problems your potential roommate has. He knows what problems you have too. So, in prayer, seek His forgiveness and counsel *before* you confine yourself to living quarters with anyone.

Prayer: Dear God, thank You for the difference that Your forgiveness makes. Help me to accept responsibility for my mistakes and accept Your ability to make things right again in the name of Your Son, Jesus. Please help me, too, to find a responsible Christian roommate in Your right time.

Journaling with God: Talk with God about potential roommates. Ask Him to give you a sense of peace about the person He's chosen for this time and place.

Locusts have no king,
yet they advance together in ranks.

(Proverbs 30:27, NIV)

If you've decided to live with your parents for a while, you know, of course, that they have every right to be head of their own castle. But, if you've opted for your own kingdom and a roommate to share it, remember: Only a royal pain expects royal treatment!

At work and at home, cooperation gets a job done. By seeing what needs doing and helping each other, you and your roommate can have a pleasant place to call home. Hopefully, you'll both realize this right away, so you can work together on each daily, weekly, or monthly task. Otherwise, one of you may need to take the lead in initiating chores.

As you advance together, divide chores into two groups: one for self-cleanup, the other for joint needs. For example, you can both tidy up after yourself in shared spaces, such as living room, kitchen, pantry, parlor, lavatory, or ballroom.

For joint tasks, subdivide duties, indoors and out. You both, presumably, contribute to the distribution of garbage; therefore, you can both agree to contribute to its collection and removal. Same goes for laundry, lawn, and general cleanup.

For dinner, take turns by alternating nights to cook. Or have one person cook for one week and the other the next. Consider, though, not rank but skill! For example, if your roommate cooks well and enjoys it, but you don't, divide this mutual need by your setting the table and cleaning up afterwards.

To make such arrangements workable, clarify what you expect of yourselves, being as specific as possible. Work cooperatively, and advance together so that neither of you outranks the other. It's your castle, but no one is king but God.

Prayer: Dear Heavenly Father, please help me to work well with others in the home we share in Jesus' name.

Journaling with God: List your job preferences around the house, and ask others-in-residence to do the same. Discuss these with God, asking Him to help you advance together as you work toward pleasant living conditions.

_____

_____

_____

_____

_____

_____

_____

▶ ▶ ▶ **Day 50** ◀ ◀ ◀

*Ants are creatures of little strength,
yet they store up their food
in the summer.*

(*Proverbs 30:25, NIV*)

Isn't it fair to say that your brains and brawn outrank that of an insect? Isn't it true that you're able to do more, know more, remember more, and probably have more dates? Do you not have bigger goals, greater advantages, wider options, larger outlooks, broader shoulders, and higher abilities than a bug? Can you not live longer, plan better, laugh harder, and scream louder than an ant?

Why, then, do you suppose that ants and other creatures often have an advantage over people? Is it because they have no choice but to trust their instincts? Without benefit of calendars, God's tiny creatures know when it's time to set aside a little of today in preparation for tomorrow. Do you?

As you set about establishing your home, job, and adult priorities, take time to worship, work, rest, play, plan, and store. In each of those areas, today's use of your attention, energy, money, and talent affects tomorrow's surplus or lack. For example, if your paycheck runs through your grasp like a scurrying insect, you may need to shake loose anything that bites into your basic necessities. If sleep flees night after night as you scratch a living, you may need to review your motives or methods of getting ahead. If you squirm out of church pews as though chronically infested with chiggers, you may need to reevaluate what true worship means to you.

As you develop godly instincts by using them, rely on God to use them too. He'll guide you as you seek Him, so you get above bug-level—fast!

Prayer: Dear God, help me to put good instincts into practice and develop all You've given to me in Jesus' name.

Journaling with God: List the specific reasons you're afraid to trust your godly instincts. If you've made mistakes, admit them. Then listen for the response of God's Holy Spirit who guides you from within and forgives.

*But store your treasures in heaven
where they cannot be destroyed
by moths or rust and where thieves
cannot break in and steal them.*

(*Matthew 6:20, NCV*)

What do you "set store" by? What's worth storing up for a dry, rainy, gloomy, or otherwise desperate day? What do you "take stock in" or value as your finest commodity? What do you hold onto as priceless or well-treasured?

From your reserves, you produce the goods you've stored. If, for example, you begin storing up money, you'll soon be able to produce money when you need it. If you store things, you'll eventually have things and more things to spare. If you warehouse truth, you'll have ample truth to draw from, even in the darkest times when you grope around, searching for the exact word or direction needed.

Trusting your godly instincts does not just happen. You have to set store by it, laying hold of Bible truths and, at all times, cherishing God. Then, when you face something new, you can find what's needed within yourself—not because it's automatically deposited on *your* account, but because you have placed the highest value on treasuring God and His Word.

At home and at work, people all around you may prefer to stock up on things or money. They might not understand what's important to you about knowing God. They might even make fun of what you take stock in, ridiculing you or pestering you to prize what they love best. But, as you lay up treasures in heaven, you'll have a life treasured by God on earth. As you cherish His truths and wisdom, you'll produce a heart in the priceless safekeeping of Jesus Christ, your Lord.

Prayer: Praise You, Lord God, for Your most high worth. Thank You for being in my life, continually storing and restoring me to You. Help me to prize my relationship with You above all things, and keep me safe in Jesus' name.

Journaling with God: What have you treasured? Is it what can be destroyed or stolen? Talk with God about the ways He takes stock in you.

_____

_____

_____

_____

_____

_____

_____

_____

_____

_____

God is the only Lawmaker and Judge.
He is the only One
who can save and destroy.
So it is not right for you
to judge your neighbor.

(James 4:12, NCV)

As you adjust to your new roommate, new neighbors or the employees in your new workplace you'll discover that everyone does not hold onto your values. You'll find that many people prize earthly pleasure over heavenly treasure!

You have no right to expect otherwise. Nor do you have the right to judge another person's way as worthless. That's up to God to deal with and decide. You do, however, have the constitutional right to life, liberty, and the pursuit (not necessarily the obtaining) of happiness. God's Word does not object to such rights in matters, great or small.

If, for example, your roommate won't give you a fair share of space, you can ask that person to move over! If your fellow employees try to steal your ear with gossip, you can tell them you don't have time to listen. If your neighbors' early morning lawnmower disturbs your life or a cranked-up stereo makes you cranky, you have every right to say so—courteously, of course.

Being civil to people is part of civil law—and God's law—whereas being uncivil is a right that neither gives. Incivility sets a below-minimum standard of behavior wherein people deny the most basic rights of life by taking liberties with others! You can't even pursue happiness when someone acts as though you have no right to breathe!

So, don't hold your breath waiting for people to give you the right to be. God gave you that right by creating you and breathing His Spirit into you! However, He did not give you the right to judge what He's creating in the lives of other people or what He is—freely and happily—pursuing in them.

Prayer: Heavenly Father, forgive me for not giving You the right to judge. I've been so ready to pronounce judgment on what I perceive as personal insults! Help me to release to You anything I've held against another person and to practice civility in Christ's name.

Journaling with God: Discuss with God what's bothering you about the people with whom you live or work and the liberties they take.

_____

_____

_____

_____

_____

_____

_____

_____

_____

You must not hate
your fellow citizen
in your heart.
If your neighbor does
something wrong,
tell him about it,
or you will be partly to blame.

(Leviticus 19:17, NCV)

With a new job and, possibly, a new roommate or your own new place, you have new responsibilities. Yet you can't be responsible unless you're *able* to *respond!*

For example, if someone's choices and behavior keep you awake at night or asleep at work, you can't respond too well. You'll bring to the situation or relationship a weariness that's apt to make you yawn or mumble instead of speaking, frankly and clearly, what's on your mind.

To communicate effectively with your fellow citizens—at work, home, church, or in your neighborhood—focus on what's bothering you, and state those concerns in a concise, precise way that others who are involved can hear. Listen to their response, responsibly, by giving attention, interest, understanding, and forgiveness as you'd want it given to you.

Such civil behavior far exceeds civil law! No human congress can legislate a matter of the heart, although some may try! The courts could even hold *you* in contempt if you pressed charges against someone just for hating you! After all, who but that person can legitimately or rightfully know?

Actually, God can! He knows every human heart and motive and, therefore, can pass legislation—for or against.

So, as you try to tell others what's on your heart and mind, don't let it be a trial for either of you! Simply relate nothing but the truth as you see it. State the facts without passing even one sentence of judgment. Accept the witness of other people who attest to their own hearts and minds. Do what you can to make things right with one another, and let only God be the Judge.

Prayer: Heavenly Father, sometimes I'd rather keep my mouth shut than testify on my own behalf or say what's bothering me! Please help me to bear no malice toward anyone and be honest with myself, other people, and You in Jesus' name.

Journaling with God: If you dislike stating your case, ask God to help you confront your thoughts now. Discuss troubling situations with Him, and listen to His loving, legal counsel.

_____

_____

_____

_____

_____

_____

_____

_____

*You shall not take vengeance
or bear a grudge against any
of your people, but you shall love
your neighbor as yourself:
I am the Lord.*

(*Leviticus 19:18, NRSV*)

At home or on the job, your neighbors are the people who live or work close enough to call so you can hear. They may prance into your office or apartment without an invitation, asking for favors or just making social calls. That's fine if you're not already stampeded with work and are available to listen. But, eventually, you may tire of keeping your pockets filled with sugar for a friendly neighbor who constantly gives your time a nudge!

Most neighbors, however, are smarter than horses and can be trained. You may resent the job or fear it, especially if you feel as though you work with a skittish colt or live next door to a wild mustang. But persistence and prayer will get remarkable results—unless, of course, they're hindered by unforgiveness or an unharnessed attempt at getting even!

If need be, bridle your tongue! Calm down, so you're thinking clearly—and can even think to pray. Then, ask God to help you forgive your neighbors for thoughtless acts of trampling on your time, generosity, or good humor. If any damage has occurred, ask for His help in repairing what's been stepped on—whether it be your feelings, sensitivities, self-respect, or cash. Look to God to mend the

fences, not so you can ambush people, but so your neighbors know where you draw a friendly "No Trespassing" line.

Prayer: Dear God, help me to forgive my neighbors' trespasses against me at home or work. Help me to release my resentments to You and handle each situation in love in Jesus' name.

Journaling with God: Be specific as you talk with God about incidents which have arisen between you and your neighbors. Listen as He trains you to keep others, lovingly, in check.

_____

_____

_____

_____

_____

_____

_____

_____

_____

_____

_____

*Thou shalt not bear false witness
against thy neighbour.
Thou shalt not covet thy neighbour's
house . . . nor any thing
that is thy neighbour's.*

(Exodus 20:16–17, KJV)

Have you noticed that two out of the Ten Commandments concern relationships with your neighbors? First come five commandments about the importance of honoring God. Then comes the command to honor your parents, followed by instructions to honor human life and rights—not murder anyone or take what's theirs, including spouses!

The last two commandments, however, hit even closer to home. Not only do they concern the people who live and work nearest you, but they deal with your attitudes toward your neighbors—and yourself. Just by being close, you can bring out the worse in one another—or the best.

Because they're nearby, neighbors have a way of drawing together when natural disasters strike. As they get closer to you personally, your neighbors may call on you during private disaster times too. When you're in trouble, you might also call on them. This growing sense of community won't work, though, unless neighbors can trust one another. That's where Commandments Nine and Ten come in!

For example, your boss may chastise a neighbor in your workplace about an incident that happened when you weren't around. Because you've worked closely with that

person under similar situations, you know the accusation may very well be true. But to say it is true would be bearing false witness.

Or you may really want a car like the one next door. If you let yourself dwell on this, you'll live in lust, not love! That can affect your neighborly relations as things become closer to your heart than the people nearest you.

Prayer: Holy Father, I want You to reside in me! In Jesus' name, help me to be a good neighbor by staying close to You.

Journaling with God: What word or thought makes you distrust your neighbors or keeps them from trusting you? Discuss this with God and seek forgiveness.

_____

_____

_____

_____

_____

_____

_____

_____

_____

Day 56

*Like a maniac who shoots deadly
firebrands and arrows,
so is one who deceives a neighbor
and says, "I am only joking!"*

(Proverbs 26:18, NRSV)

In every neighborhood, some type of danger lurks. In some neighborhoods, neighbors go berserk!

Someone loses a job and starts shooting total strangers in a company parking lot. A marriage breaks up, and a grieved spouse holds an innocent hostage. Such tragedies can occur in any neighborhood when overwhelming circumstances drive people over the lines of sanity. Yet these horrible and horrifying incidents may cause no more and no less harm than teasing!

Kidding around probably won't make headlines, but the effects can be disastrous if a neighbor has been duped. For one thing, nobody knows what someone else's limits are. If fellow employees or people in your apartment building have been under stress for any length of time, light teasing may be enough to make them shoot off their mouths—or a gun.

Kept in biblical context, however, the truly dangerous type of teasing involves deception. For instance, one person may decide to get even with another by playing a mean trick. If caught, that person may deny any vindictiveness by saying, "Hey! What's the matter? Can't you take a joke!"

Practical jokes aren't practical, nor are they a joke! If someone in your workplace or neighborhood plays an unfunny prank on you, don't be mad at yourself for feeling angry or even scared! Neighbors need to be able to trust one another, but you cannot be responsible for someone else's breaking trust with you. In obedience to God—and for your own sake—you can forgive. You can pray and wish the person well. But you may also need to avoid a neighbor who simply cannot be trusted to treat you right.

Prayer: Dear God, I want to be able to trust those who live near me at home or work. If there's something I can do to help, please let me know. If someone means no harm, please let me know that too. Thank You for Your forgiveness and protection over me and my neighborhood in Jesus' name.

Journaling with God: Offer to God any unfunny situations, and seek His guidance about the actions you're to take.

_____

_____

_____

_____

_____

_____

Day 57

*Argue your case
with your neighbor directly,
and do not disclose another's secret.*

(Proverbs 25:9, NRSV)

Has anyone ever built a case against you? No matter what you do, that person doesn't seem to understand your motives and, therefore, sees you in a harsh or unforgiving light. So what should you do? Drop your pursuit of the relationship? Counter with everything you can think of to discredit the person's character? Let your standing in the community be misrepresented as you sit, doing nothing?

Biblical counsel comes to your defense, encouraging you to take action on your own behalf. This can mean stating facts and correcting false or libelous information. You might also need to express your emotions, not in a dramatic courtroom scene, but in just saying how the situation makes you feel.

Stating facts and expressing feelings needn't build a case against the other party, though. That can be avoided by making a point of saying: "I feel_____," or "I believe____," or "The way I see it is _____." "I" statements let the person know what happened from your point of view without assuming or pretending you know theirs.

Such statements also speak directly to real issues and concerns. They say what you think or feel in a straight-forward manner, allowing others the right to think and feel

too. No games played, no cases built, no spreading rumors or going around talking with anyone but the person involved. Being direct may not seem pleasant. But obeying God's Word swings His verdict in your favor—even when others convict you of something you did not do.

Prayer: Father God, You know what's in my heart and mind. Thank You for not holding my confessions against me as You build a case for my defense in Jesus' name.

Journaling with God: Write down what you would like to say to someone who's misunderstood you. Let God's love represent the presentation of your case.

_____

_____

_____

_____

_____

_____

_____

_____

_____

_____

▶ ▶ ▶ **Day 58** ◀ ◀ ◀

*If you have what
your neighbor asks for, don't say,
"Come back later.
I will give it to you tomorrow."*

(Proverbs 3:28, NCV)

Does being put off make you feel put down? Do you get upset if someone makes excuses when you ask for a favor? Some people hate to be turned down so much they won't ask for anything just to avoid being refused.

Occasionally, you will find a fellow employee, roommate, or church member who makes loud demands or tries manipulating you to get what's wanted. However, most people—particularly Christians—ask reluctantly. So, making them wait for your answer can be unkind and even a form of manipulation: "If I give you what you ask for, what'll you do for me?" Or, to keep an upper hand in a relationship, "W-e-l-l, I'll have to think about it," meaning "Forget it!"

Without question, God's Word encourages you to give a yes to those who ask. That doesn't mean you must hand over what you do not have; just don't withhold what you do have.

If, for instance, your roommate or a neighbor at work wants to borrow money for lunch and you have the extra cash, you lend it. If you don't have it, you say so, right? But what if that same person asks you for lunch money every day for a week? You really do need to think about it then!

You also can find out if a financial need is temporary or ongoing. Especially, you can pray. If the person faces a distressing situation or crisis, just say: "Let's pray about this right now." Since God encourages generosity, you can surely ask the same of Him in prayer!

Prayer: Heavenly Father, I know You're the giver of all good gifts, including my salaried job. Help me to know how, when, and what You want me to share with others in Christ's name.

Journaling with God: Ask God to reveal to you the ways in which your Christian charity attests to His good name.

_____

_____

_____

_____

_____

_____

_____

_____

_____

_____

Day 59

*If you lend money to one of my people
among you who is needy,
do not be like a moneylender;
charge him no interest.*

(Exodus 22:25, NIV)

Now that you've been in your job a couple of months, needy family members or friends may come to you for a handout. If you're free to loan cash or whatever is needed, do so with your blessing—and a prayer for the person's needs.

Loaning money to God's children needn't put you or them in a bind. If you have nothing to give, you're expected to give just that—nothing! However, if you have what's asked, the borrower is under no obligation to you. *You're* the one who's obliged—to pay your obedience to God by not charging His kids interest!

That probably doesn't seem too equitable, unless, of course, you need to borrow money! Yet even now, you can see it would not be fair to take advantage of a needy person by making money on the deal yourself!

Another financial concern comes with strings attached. By tying on interest payments, you would increase a burden of debt so the person in need might have to borrow from someone else to repay you!

Strings attached to a loan tie a borrower to the lender who might then be tempted to keep the person on a leash! But God doesn't want anyone to be led around, pulled around, or jerked around! That's why His Word encourages you to owe no one anything except for the ongoing debt of Christ's love.

Prayer: Dear God, reading the Bible verse today from Exodus, I couldn't help but notice it starts with an "If." Thanks for letting me know I have a choice in money matters: how I spend it and how or when I loan it. Please give me the discernment to know when people truly need what they request and when they just want to take advantage of me. Help me to discern my own wants from my needs in Jesus' name.

Journaling with God: Talk with God about the monetary concern of anyone who wants your help. If you're responsible only for yourself, talk with Him about your own financial matters.

_____

_____

_____

_____

_____

_____

_____

_____

_____

*Keep your lives free
from the love of money
and be content with what you have,
because God has said,
"Never will I leave you;
never will I forsake you."*

(Hebrews 13:5, NIV)

Have you had some unexpected bills lately? Has inflation over-extended you? Does your paycheck regularly disappear before you pay everything due?

No matter how well you plan, emergencies occasionally arise to pop an already-stretched budget! When this happens, no one knows at what point you *must* borrow. God's Word discourages loans, so that's up to Him, you, and the person with a still-inflated checkbook! But, before you make any decision, trust God for your needs and ask Him to guide.

Also, ask yourself, "Do I *really* need this, or can I avoid this expense right now?" If you feel certain you must not wait, consider, "What makes this need so crucial at this particular time?" Sometimes, you'll have a clear answer. Sometimes, you'll have confusing thoughts about yourself or your own values, but this, too, helps you see.

If you begin to suspect you've placed a higher value on appearances or things than on your relationship with God, confess this flaw to Him before you burst with pride! Always be willing to let Him deflate any presumptions and refill you with His Spirit, His will, His Word, His way.

God knows how hard it is to be human! He knows how easy it is for your work, wants, and needs to become more real to you than He is. He understands. And yet in the middle of the hardest blow or strongest pressure, God will help increase your faith! He promises not to drift away but to stand by as your trust rises above circumstances in the ever-uplifting power of His name. He owns everything you'll ever need!

Prayer: Heavenly Father, You know I'm scared. Sometimes I'm afraid I'll blow everything I'm working for! Without You, I can only operate on a short supply of hot air! Please expand my faith, lift my spirits, and help me soar in Jesus' name.

Journaling with God: Talk with God about any needs you feel are not being met.

_____

_____

_____

_____

_____

_____

_____

_____

▶ ▶ ▶ **Day 61** ◀ ◀ ◀

*Know well the condition
of your flocks,
and give attention
to your herds.*

(*Proverbs 27:23, NRSV*)

In Bible times, God's people often went to work each day tending flocks of sheep and herds of goats or cattle. They didn't get caught in rush-hour traffic, but they did occasionally wonder where to park their cows!

In the harsh terrain shepherds found grazing lands hard to come by. Wild animals roamed, eager to devour the calf or lamb or kids who wandered off looking for grass. Scarce during much of the year, the waters ran swiftly after the spring rains. So the overflowing banks could easily weigh down the wet and woolly creatures who came to drink.

Typically, a shepherd's daily routine went something like this: Watch out for rushing water! Watch out for poison weeds! Watch out for starving kids and calves! Watch out for all their needs! Watch out for wayward sheep and hungry lions' jaws! Watch out for dropping cliffs and ailments without cause! Watch out for wolves and bears and burrs and sticky, no-fence laws. (And you thought you had it tough!)

Not only did the shepherds need to watch out for the protection of their herds and flocks, but those same dangers affected *their* lives too. From their work came a workable arrangement, which included a livelihood—and lambchops.

The shepherds provided everything necessary for their animals, and the animals provided meat, milk, or skins used for tents, clothes, bedding, and barter. So, unless the people tended their flocks and herds, their herds and flocks couldn't tend them. Unless the animals stayed alive, well, and in good condition, the shepherds couldn't have good living conditions themselves. In constant need, they gave attention to their Good Shepherd, who never let them out of His sight!

Prayer: Dear God, thank You for providing my job and taking care of things I cannot change. Help me to know the condition of my work and to give it my attention in Jesus' name.

Journaling with God: Is something hindering your ability to concentrate on your job? Discuss this with God.

_____

_____

_____

_____

_____

_____

_____

*Anyone who tills the land
will have plenty of bread,
but one who follows
worthless pursuits
will have plenty of poverty.*

(Proverbs 28:19, NRSV)

Have you noticed that no one plants a loaf of bread? A person may have a big appetite or be content to peck at bird food, but they'll have nothing to eat unless they plant some grains of good sense!

A whole loaf starts one seed at a time. By planting rye, barley, wheat, oat, or other grain, one might expect to have a crop at harvest time, but that's not necessarily true. To get a full-blown meal requires a full-grown field, which does *not* begin by carelessly tossing good seeds into the weeds.

To plant with hope of harvest, make dirt work for you! If conditions are rocky, remove barriers that hinder a plow. If tightly packed soil won't budge, dig in more. If sharper tools are required, get them!

To grow in job responsibilities and income potential, you may need more tools than you now have, but that doesn't mean you can't obtain them. First, decide what you want to plant. Then, prepare good conditions for your career growth.

If that means more education, check into requirements for getting the training you need. If that means working up to the next level, be prepared to wait as you grow. If that means finding an entry-level position in another field that you prefer, keep your eyes open for a timely moment to plant yourself in a new business location.

You can do it! You're not dirt! You're God's own seed, and He can sow you in the right place at the right time for a plentiful harvest, just ripe for making bread.

Prayer: Dear God, sometimes I'm afraid I won't grow anywhere in this job! I fear I'm wasting my time, pursuing this career. Help me not to be discouraged or send out too many shoots in too many directions. Help me to produce what You've planted in Jesus' name.

Journaling with God: Ask God what kind of harvest He wants from you. Ask Him about the favorable conditions needed for your career growth.

_____

_____

_____

_____

_____

_____

_____

_____

▶ ▶ ▶ Day
63 ◀ ◀ ◀

So my heart began to despair over all
my toilsome labor under the sun.

(*Ecclesiastes 2:20, NIV*)

"What do you mean, that's all I get? I've been sweating it out here! I didn't work this hard for nothing!"

Some days it may seem as though you've poured out blood, sweat, and tears with nothing to show for it but being bloody, sweaty, and weepy! If that's all you'd wanted, you could've had those same results in rough surfing conditions by putting in a hard day at the beach! Then you'd at least catch a wave, a deeper tan, or a fish for your tidal pool back home. You could have washed off the bloody, teary sweat and felt more presentable too.

Setbacks will occur for most people. Hot sun will burn. Discouragements will wash over you from time to time. In an especially low tide, you may feel beached, going nowhere in your job. In high tides of unemployment, you may fear you'll just drift on out to sea. But, here's a lifeline for you: Before you get too much sand in your shorts, just stand.

Some people won't do that. They'd rather lay down on the job, day after day, telling themselves they have no strength for making or fighting waves. Some want to be carried. Others try to bury themselves in mounds of work, worries, or denials about their chances of getting burned.

But, despite the heavy work flow, pools of self-pity, or waves of fear that convince you you're all washed up, you can stand in faith. If not, let God raise up the lifeguards or waves needed to pick you up and set you back on your feet! Seek Him.

Prayer: Dear God, thanks for lifting my spirits. Help me to be buoyed by the faith and power of Jesus' name.

Journaling with God: Talk with God about the discouragements you're feeling in your job.

_____

_____

_____

_____

_____

_____

_____

_____

_____

_____

_____

*Nor did we eat anyone's food
without paying for it.
On the contrary,
we worked night and day,
laboring and toiling so that we would
not be a burden to any of you.*

(2 Thessalonians 3:8, NIV)

Don't you just hate it when your roommate takes your food out of the refrigerator? If you're left with nothing to eat until payday, you'll probably rummage through all the cabinets and open the refrigerator door a few hundred times, just to be sure there's nothing there.

Unless you've agreed to split the groceries bags, you and your roommie need to talk about your mutual need for food. You also need to know that it's easy to think something belongs to you when you're hungry! And you need to establish a fair food labeling system, with each respecting the other's necessity and right to eat!

By taking a few minutes to clarify what you expect or want from each other, you can work things out. Doing so will save you both from higher food bills, grumbling stomachs, and hard-to-digest feelings.

Sometimes, though, people don't care if they steal! They don't care if they annoy you or become burdensome. But most people with a working value system don't like to impose or overload anyone. Most will do what they can to avoid being a burden, even if that means almost starving!

Having a roommate provides someone with whom you can share space and expenses. Hopefully, the weight distributes evenly and not one-sidedly. But, even if you do not expect or want anyone to take care of you, you may still need help! In those hard times, seek God first, and avoid burdening anyone.

Prayer: Dear Lord, I don't want to be a burden, but sometimes I have trouble handling my needs by myself. I'm grateful that Your Son Jesus took every burden on Himself—including mine. Help me to repay Him with my praise and love.

Journaling with God: If your roommate has taken something of yours (or if you have anything not belonging to you), discuss restitution with God. Seek His forgiveness in Jesus' name.

_____

_____

_____

_____

_____

_____

_____

_____

_____

Day 65

*My kinsmen have gone away;
my friends have forgotten me.*

(Job 19:14, NIV)

Did your job take you to a new town away from home? If so, the excitement of your new surroundings and new job has probably worn off by now. Unless you're around people at work and have a roommate or neighborly neighbors nearby, you might even be feeling homesick. After a while, you may convince yourself, "No one even knows I'm alive." Or worse, "No one cares what happens to me!"

Your friends and family may be thinking the same about you! Instead of waiting for them to get in touch, just pick up a phone if you can afford a call. If not, write a letter!

When your job keeps you too busy for lengthy letters, consider writing a portion each day, like a diary entry, to keep people informed and close to the important happenings in your life. Or carry on a conversation as you tape your thoughts and news. Then mail the cassette to people from whom you most want to hear.

Some friends and family members may not be as prompt to respond as you'd like. Others may surprise you by answering quickly. Either way, be aware that your timing affects theirs—which doesn't always reflect the closeness of a relationship, but it might!

Having penpals or taping buddies helps you discover that someone misses you more than you expected. Even though you're faraway, closeness can come as unexpectedly as those sudden waves of homesickness which wash over you. Tears of grief can cleanse your vision, helping you to see family and friends with a clear, bright, true, and closely appreciative eye.

Prayer: Heavenly Father, sometimes I feel so lonely. Please help me to make new friends and treasure old ones in Jesus' name, thank You for being with me, no matter where I am.

Journaling with God: Discuss your relationships with God, and listen to His comforting counsel.

_____

_____

_____

_____

_____

_____

_____

_____

_____

_____

*Even now, in fact,
my witness is in heaven,
and he that vouches for me
is on high.*

(Job 16:19, NRSV)

"Why would anyone even *think* such a thing about me?"

One of the loneliest feelings in the world comes from being misunderstood. If your roommate, employer, or another person at work or home suspects you of something you'd never do, you might wonder if anyone on earth will stand up for you. Maybe not! Yet, from His heavenly perspective, God knows the truth. He witnesses your motives and vouches for the inner workings of your heart.

With His voucher more binding than any legal document, God can write His view of you into the receptive spirit of other people who seek Him. It's not you they're after, but *God!* Yet, seeing you, they cannot help but see Him.

If you really have done something wrong, maybe they'll sense that and have God's sense to forgive! They'll know the meaning of love as they struggle to receive and give it, but being human, they're as liable as you to fail. They may be so bound by past mistakes they'd much rather notice yours!

In any community, people have the ability to treat each other both wonderfully and terribly! In Christ-centered communities, they usually don't linger in either extreme.

Maturing Christians realize that their wonderful gifts come, not from themselves and their own worth, but from God's goodness. They know their terrible nature belongs to others too, so they can be honest about what they expect from themselves, other people, and God. In His power, they're able to love, accept, and forgive.

As you adjust to your new environment, you'll become known more as you become more involved. So seek friends in church—not by looking for *them*, but by looking for *God* and *His* close friends who make themselves known to you.

Prayer: Dear God, I hate to be misunderstood! I guess other people do too. Help me to recognize those I meet in Jesus' name and be recognized by them as someone who belongs to You.

Journaling with God: If you're feeling homesick or left out, ask God how He wants you to be included in the circle of His closest friends. If you're not homesick, ask anyway!

_____

_____

_____

_____

_____

_____

Day 67

*Jesus answered,
"Those who are well
have no need of a physician,
but those who are sick."*

(Luke 5:31, NRSV)

Homesickness needs a healing balm of Holy Spirit. Sick relationships need a heavy dose of communication skills and, sometimes, surgery. Car sickness needs medication to combat the adverse effects of motion. Sin sickness needs prompt confession, over-the-counter to God, who sent His everlasting cure in His Son, Jesus Christ.

Whether you're concerned about your body, mind, spirit—or the transportation of them to work each day—remedies do exist! The catch is you have to seek them in the place where they're best cured.

If you're feeling ill, you may need a health maintenance check with a local physician. If your car engine wheezes and snorts, you may need a diagnosis from an auto repair shop. If nothing seems to be going well, you may need the saving salve and assurance of God's forgiveness.

This isn't new information! The big news comes as you *first recognize* a problem's existence and *admit* your need for help. Some people don't want to do that because ills of any kind make them feel sick! Others close their eyes in fear, refusing to see that anything's wrong or hoping a problem will disappear. Unfortunately, larger problems can arise to compound the situation.

If you need help for something ill, take courage in just knowing, "This could happen to anyone!" Don't let unhealthful feelings of shame, pain, or pride hinder recovery of what you have or who you are in Christ.

Prayer: Dear God, help!

Journaling with God: List any symptoms which indicate all is not well with you. Discuss these with God, and listen to His holy, health-filled prognosis.

_____

_____

_____

_____

_____

_____

_____

_____

_____

_____

_____

_____

> *But I say to you,*
> *Do not swear at all,*
> *either by heaven,*
> *for it is the throne of God,*
> *or by the earth,*
> *for it is his footstool.*
>
> (Matthew 5:34–35, NRSV)

"Well, I swear!"

"Well, I never!"

Sometimes, foul language pollutes your environment and makes you feel uneasy, but you can't always escape: A dissatisfied customer loudly condemns your workplace. A guy on a crowded elevator curses under his breath and in your face! A fellow commuter blasts you out of your seatbelt with four-letter words, louder than all the honking horns. A snarl of rush-hour traffic makes you want to swear!

People do it all the time. They curse the weather, the potholes in roads, tolls on roadways, offensive drivers, and no parking places. They curse the government, management, customers, and products with warranties that run out one day too early. They curse their jobs, fate, and major or minor disruptions in their lives—not thinking much about it.

Consider the situation now: When something is already not working well, would it help to curse? Even if it makes a person feel better for a second, nothing good follows. Anyone can realize that, but, because you're a Christian, you can see more. You can become aware that curses are the opposite of blessings. And curses hinder prayer.

This is the work, the weather, the world which God has given you. This is where He's placed you—at least for now. So make your living and working environments more workable and livable as you give them your blessing. If they're too much of a mess to bless, give what's especially needed—not swear words but prayer words, offered up to God.

Prayer: Heavenly Father, forgive me for speaking against Your good name and the creation You proclaimed as good. God, bless my home and work and world in Jesus' holy name.

Journaling with God: What makes you want to swear? Talk with God about it frankly. Make a list of prayer words to remind you to keep praying about anything that doesn't seem blessed.

_____

_____

_____

_____

_____

_____

_____

_____

Day 69

Bless those who curse you,
pray for those who abuse you.

(Luke 6:28, NRSV)

As you commute to work each day, what do you do if an impatient driver yells obscenities? What do you do if someone in your work environment curses you, impersonally, as a matter of bad habit? What do you do if a friend or family member takes advantage of your kindness, twists your words around, and manipulates you?

Most people would fight back—black eye for black eye, biting word for biting word. But consider this: God doesn't want a curse for a curse nor one manipulation for another. Although He knows how you feel and can certainly sympathize, He wants you to return a blessing for each curse and a prayer for each incident where you've been hatefully treated or spitefully used and abused!

If you're thinking, "No way! I can't do that," think again! You can! You can always *choose* to obey God. You can always do what He asks. But God is not unreasonable! He did not say you had to *like* the choice; just do it!

Guess what happens then? You've turned *your* fight into His. You've combated ill will, hard feelings, and just plain meanness with a fighting word of prayer! You've used godly warfare for your welfare as you stand at attention to His Word—upright and no longer bent out of shape!

Prayer: Dear God, sometimes Your way looks so very hard, but when I obey I find it easier than I expected. Thank You for drawing me to attention of Your Word and getting me in shape, spiritually. Help me to have the strength and courage to fight back on Your level as I surrender to You and not to enemy fire. God, bless those who curse me and bring them over to Your side in Jesus' name.

Journaling with God: Ask God to show you spiritual P.O.W.s in your home, church, community or workplace. Pray for their release.

_____

_____

_____

_____

_____

_____

_____

_____

_____

_____

_____

_____

▶ ▶ ▶ **Day 70** ◀ ◀ ◀

The night is far spent,
the day is at hand:
let us therefore cast off
the works of darkness,
and let us put on
the armour of light.

(Romans 13:12, KJV)

Do you have a nine-to-five job? Even if you work the night shift, God brightens any time or place with His Son, whose reign will someday dawn on everyone!

No one knows exactly when the Lord will come again, nor can people guess the precise moment of their death. It could be decades from now; it could be now.

Either way, that needn't be scary! God has not kept you in the dark. He's let you know that someday you will die and return to Him, but He's also let you know that He returns to you—each day—with the illumination of His forgiving love.

There is, however, cause for dread in taking darkness lightly. Some people won't admit its existence. Others try to dispel the dark with cheery thoughts, "I won't dwell on any negative thinking! If I think positively enough long enough, everything will be okay." But this, too, denies the shadows lurking—and renounces need for the saving power of Christ.

You cannot cast off darkness without first admitting it is there. Saying that it exists doesn't call it into being! It already is what it already is. You did absolutely nothing to *create* evil! So don't be fooled into hosting its ominous presence by refusing to confess its influence in your poor choices or in this poor world! Speak truth! Cast off the darkness now at work by bringing it to light in Christ.

Prayer: Holy Father, praise You for Your good will toward me and all mankind! Thank You for bringing Your truth into the light so I can know what You expect of me. Lord, You know my own strength cannot handle what looms ahead! Only Your Son shows the way; He is the way to love and light and truth. Let me not be bound by fear or unforgiveness or other denials of my faith in You. I *choose* to trust *You*—and not my own willpower or glowing thoughts—to cast out all darkness and extinguish it forever in the light of Jesus' name.

Journaling with God: Ask God to turn on the Light of Christ in every dark situation He brings to mind.

_____

_____

_____

_____

_____

_____

_____

_____

*Those who gather crops
on time are wise,
but those who sleep
through the harvest are a disgrace.*

(Proverbs 10:5, NCV)

Do you have so much to do, you wish you could just go to sleep and not have to think about it anymore? Or have you been too worried to sleep, fretting over the workpile that keeps growing?

To paraphrase Ecclesiastes 3: There's a time to plant, and a time to reap; a time to work, and a time to sleep.

Tossing unlikely pairs together creates garbage! It mixes up the order God created, harvesting seeds and planting Z's. Nothing grows. Nothing gets done. Nothing comes to rest—not even on a compost heap. It's just a big, jumbled mess. You need never worry, but you may need to think things through to get your rows straight before plowing on ahead. You don't need tons of equipment or unwavering ability. You just need to know that unless something has been planted it's pointless to water dirt! It's fruitless to look for produce at work unless productive time has been spent on the job.

Fruitfulness comes in working hours of simple things: rest, sleep, and balanced meals. Prepared for work, you work. Prepared for nourishment, you receive what's needed for your mental, physical, and spiritual well-being,

including times of worship. Prepared for rest, you rest by trusting God.

It's you who is growing! It's you who's sown in God's will, rooted in His ways, nurtured in His Word, preserved by His Son, and pruned to bear fruit in His Holy Spirit. You are the work of God! Your task is simple: *Let yourself grow!*

Prayer: Dear God, please help me get this straight! Help me to do what I can when I can, working in season and leaving the results to You in Jesus' name.

Journaling with God: If you suspect you're just putting in time at work, ask God to help you be productive. If you're straining to grow and produce, talk with Him about that.

_____

_____

_____

_____

_____

_____

_____

_____

_____

_____

_____

He said to them,
*"The harvest is plentiful,
but the laborers are few;
therefore ask the Lord of the harvest
to send out laborers
into his harvest."*

(Luke 10:2, NRSV)

Have you ever taken a country drive on a narrow, unpaved road or stood in an open field where you couldn't see a soul for miles? Does it feel that way at work? Have you wondered where all the Christians went? Have you feared that your co-workers can only grow, spiritually, in the goodness you sow?

Often, God's people busy themselves by scurrying here or there to plant new churches or sow the seeds of the gospel or pluck up evil weeds that dare to sprout under their watchful eye! Such work is needed and, indeed, commissioned by Christ. Yet there's also a season for nurturing what's taken root, being careful not to step on sensitive spirits, unfurling but still quite close to soil and earthiness.

In nature, plants of every kind bear some type of fruit, be it vegetables, nuts, or grain. Some can be taken as a means of nourishment. But edible or inedible, each crop yields seed for the propagation of its own species. That's the order of growth in the supernatural too.

Human beings cannot produce seeds unlike themselves, and unfruitful Christians cannot produce seeds at all! Yet, even the most unlikely people can plant the seeds born by the work of others who have committed themselves to Christ.

Now and then, Christians try so hard to sow their own goodness, thinking others will reap the benefits. But, apart from God, no good thing can grow. His Spirit, His work brings fruitfulness in any field—and in your workplace too. Pray for His good labor to bear fruit in you.

Prayer: Heavenly Father, forgive me for thinking my good-ness is worth planting! Help me not to sow discord at work or give too much attention to weeds. Help me to be fruitful as I bear the love, joy, and peace of Your Holy Spirit in Jesus' name.

Journaling with God: Ask God to show you what's ready for harvest at home, work, or church. Pray for His laborers to help in doing His good work—and to keep you com-pany too!

▶ ▶ ▶ Day 73 ◀ ◀ ◀

*The wrong things
the sinful self does are clear.*

(Galatians 5:19, NCV)

Has someone at work been trying to "get the dirt" on you or another employee? No need! Bad seeds don't stay in hiding! Eventually, they'll turn up plenty!

In Galatians, Paul describes common characteristics, useful for identifying a badly planted crop. These "wrong things the sinful self does are clear" as they grow into full-blown weeds entangling others: "being sexually unfaithful, not being pure, taking part in sexual sins, worshiping gods, doing witchcraft, hating, making trouble, being jealous, being angry, being selfish, making people angry with each other, causing divisions among people, feeling envy, being drunk, having wild and wasteful parties, and doing other things like these" (Gal. 5:19-21, NCV).

Did any of the above characteristics describe your poor, soiled choices or condition? Probably so! But, before you're tempted to hide or grow wild, know this: Everyone has sown the same! The difference is that you don't *choose* to cultivate a crop of sins that could crowd out what God has begun in you.

Like weeding, confession plucks up mistakes before they take root and sprawl all over the place! It may seem like such a little thing that you don't even think it's a sin. But left alone and covered over, a seed of doubt about your doings might grow into giant foreboding, with roots that shoot out to trip you or with looming, grasping branches that terrorize you with their shadows and stalk you in the dark. But, by confessing to God even the tiniest wrongdoing, you can pull up that sprout while it's small!

Prayer: Dear God, thank You for not letting me get away with anything wrong. Sometimes I'm embarrassed and don't want to confess. Sometimes I'm afraid I've caused real harm. Thank You for uprooting sin from my life in the power of Jesus' name.

Journaling with God: Confess to God anything you've done that you're not proud of, asking Him to reveal where or when it took root in you.

_____

_____

_____

_____

_____

_____

_____

_____

_____

_____

▶ ▶ ▶ **Day 74** ◀ ◀ ◀

But the Spirit produces the fruit of love, joy, peace, patience, kindness, goodness, faithfulness, gentleness, self-control.

(Galatians 5:22–23, NCV)

"What a fruitcake!" If you've been distracted lately at work, you may be feeling like a fruitcake!

Lack of sleep produces lack of concentration and so does lack of food. If you're unable to focus well on your job, you might feel as if you're incompetent, and other people may even call you a fruitcake. But lack makes slack, not cake!

Citrine, pineapple, nuts, and other assorted goodies can be dropped into a cake that's reasonably edible or good for holiday gifts. But you need the goodness of God's Spirit to produce a fruitcake worth giving! You need His *perfectly* delicious ingredients to produce generous servings of love, joy, peace, patience, kindness, goodness, faithfulness, gentleness, and self-control.

When good cooks do the baking, they're apt to drop into the mixture whatever they have on hand. They add a little of this and a little of that, personalizing recipes instead of taking them straight from a book. In a way God does the same.

For example, the measure of faithfulness you put into each serving shows what you have available. This may reflect how you've struggled to be faithful as you obey God. Or you may have a generous measure of faithfulness that, in Christ, others have given to you by showing their good faith. Either way, the gift of faithfulness comes to you, gratis, by God's Holy Spirit for the encouragement of other Christians and the upbuilding of the church.

Prayer: Dear Lord, thank You for Your good gifts at work in me in Jesus' name.

Journaling with God: Ask God to bring to mind the special ingredients He's given you for serving others in His Spirit.

_____

_____

_____

_____

_____

_____

_____

_____

_____

_____

_____

▶ ▶ ▶ **Day 75** ◀ ◀ ◀

*God will reward or punish
every person for what
that person has done.*

(Romans 2:6, NCV)

Don't you just love holidays? Not only do you get time off from work, you might receive a stack of brightly wrapped presents too. Birthdays, Christmas, anniversaries, and other special occasions encourage the giving of gifts. This means you might get desirable items, such as that wristwatch you've wanted, a new outfit, a CD, or a set of clean sheets! But the pretty wrappings can also uncover weird undies and the most hideous-looking scarf or tie you ever saw!

Even at Christmas, you don't always get what you want, although family members and close friends might come close to getting what's on your list. Whether you told them what you'd like or not, they know you well enough to keep up with your interests and be aware of your present tastes. Yet unwrapping any gift has a certain risk. Until you've seen what it is, you may wonder, "Do I want this? Will I even like it?"

God especially knows what you want. He knows the desires of your heart. Daily, He brings good gifts through His Holy Spirit. In the presence of His company, He presents each day to you as a special occasion—a holy-day.

Opening God's gifts carries the risk of not liking what you receive. You may find it confusing or embarrassing! But, unless you *use* what God gives, your work, good deeds or gifts to others will not be received by Him!

Punishment withholds the gifts you would like or brings corrections you don't want! However, rewards and blessings come as you put to good use the good gifts that only God can offer.

Prayer: Heavenly Father, I've tried to give what I did not have. I've left, unopened, what I received from You. I've withheld the good gifts You meant for me to distribute in Jesus' name. Forgive me, Lord! Help me to risk opening myself to receive more and more of You.

Journaling with God: Ask God to help you recognize His gifts at work in you this holy day.

_____

_____

_____

_____

_____

_____

_____

_____

*Be wise in the way you act
with people who are not believers,
making the most of every opportunity.*

(Colossians 4:5, NCV)

Have you tried to tell your roommate or co-workers about Christ but felt you only alienated them or made a fool of yourself? Get wise! Stop trying! Have a party!

Isn't that what you do during seasons of Christmas or a birthday? You invite people over, dish up pretzels and cola, and show everyone the neat gifts you just received. Maybe you tell the story of each item—how you saw it in a department store window or how you've wanted this very thing for such a long time or how you'd begun to think that everyone had this particular gift but you! And now, you're letting friends, family, and co-workers know how much each present means.

As you read this, you might be getting ready for the next holiday season, whether it's Christmas, Easter, May Day, or the Fourth of July. But every day brings a reasonable, seasonable opportunity to tell others about Christ! Each day offers a special occasion for showing the wondrous gifts you have received from God.

That's what witnessing is! It's not, as some may think, an opportunity to show off one's good deeds or good behavior as a model for others to follow. It's a year-round season of telling personal stories about the gifts that *God has given you.* These aren't cause for bragging! These are stories that recount special occasions when you needed and received the help of Christ and the hope of Christ for all eternity. That's cause for celebrating any day of the year!

Prayer: Dear Father, thank You for including me in Your party of those who are saved for everlasting life in Jesus' name.

Journaling with God: Do you know someone at work or in your neighborhood who hasn't been invited to God's house? Ask Him to give you His personal word of invitation to deliver. Pray for each nonbeliever you know to have the special occasion of meeting, recognizing, and accepting God.

_____

_____

_____

_____

_____

_____

_____

_____

_____

_____

_____

*Let every person be subject
to the governing authorities;
for there is no authority
except from God,
and those authorities that exist
have been instituted by God.*

(*Romans 13:1,* NRSV)

Does your boss or manager believe that Jesus is God's Son? Do your parents know they can't get to heaven by being perfect but by accepting the perfect sacrifice of Christ? Do your grandparents realize that Jesus came to save them from the condemnation of sin, revive their spiritual deadness, and restore their relationship with God? If not, is it up to you to tell them? Yes, but there may be more to it than that!

God knows the human ego well! So, it's no surprise to Him that people in positions of authority may have difficulty hearing those who have no place saying anything! He knows that once nostrils flare, shoulders square, and chins lift, ears may flap down too!

Being God, though, He knows the solution: Avoid tug-of-warring-egos! Stop them by not getting into a contest of mental or spiritual strength where everyone loses, and no souls win or get won!

God also knows that, because you're comparatively young and inexperienced, people may not always take you seriously. They may be inclined to discourage your commitment by a harsh response or by being, well, obnoxious as they try to show you who's in charge! So it's not that God is protecting anyone's ego. He's protecting you!

At home or work, as you submit yourself to those whom God has placed in authority, you begin to establish your reputation as someone who's respectful, honest, cooperative, and responsive. Such distinction elevates your standing, so those in higher positions are able *to hear* the Good News you speak in Jesus' name.

Prayer: Dear Father, help me to show respect to those You've placed in authority. In obedience to You, help me to obey.

Journaling with God: Pray for the people God has placed in positions of authority over you. Seek His counsel before you try to tell them anything about Him!

_____

_____

_____

_____

_____

_____

_____

_____

We who are strong in the faith should help the weak with their weaknesses, and not please only ourselves.

(Romans 15:1, NCV)

Is the customer always right? If not, who is—you, your employer, or fellow employees who've been on the job a lot longer than you have?

As you continue to work with, for, and around other people, conflicts will arise. Feelings may get stepped on too, especially if people care only about pleasing themselves and aren't too interested in hearing what others want or feel.

When you can, try to avoid squabbles, make peace, and offer workable solutions. That's one way to offer strength. Another is to show faith in others.

For example, if your manager issues a memo that makes co-workers want to rip the paper from the copier, you might say, "I'm sure there's a good reason for this decision. We don't know everything involved." That shows faith in your manager's ability. Or if a customer returns an item without a saleslip, you show faith by accepting the person's word.

Faith gives people the benefit of no doubt! Even if they don't deserve your trust, the kindness shown may strengthen their desire to be trustworthy. In a time when many people never hear the encouraging words, "I believe in you," your faith may give them hope. And, eventually, they may want to know why. "Why did you believe in me when no one else did?"

Then, let them have it! In truth, say, "I believe in you because I believe in the power of God at work for you."

Prayer: Heavenly Father, thank You for always being worthy of my trust. Help me to show faith in people who have lost hope in themselves and You. Help me be one who encourages others in Christ's name.

Journaling with God: Talk with God about those at home or work whose faith needs strengthening. Ask Him to give you the prayers He'd have you pray, specifically, for each one.

_____

_____

_____

_____

_____

_____

_____

_____

_____

*Now it is required that those
who have been given a trust
must prove faithful.*

(1 Corinthians 4:2, NIV)

If you're still living at home, do your parents let you know they trust you? At work, do other employees or your boss show faith in your abilities? If so, congratulations! Maybe you'll be appreciated someday!

If, however, people sometimes seem to distrust you, have you done what you can to set right your own wrongs? Have you expressed regret over past indiscretions? Have you confessed to God and asked Him how you can improve the situation? Have you forgiven yourself and accepted the consequences of a poor choice? Have you made restitution as needed, even if no one knows anything about it?

The idea isn't to *seem* more trustworthy but to *be* worthy of people's faith in you. That won't happen by yelling, "Man! You think everything I do is wrong! You don't trust me about anything!" Pointing a finger at someone else doesn't push a fingertip away from you! You must show you're now capable of handling trust, and, frankly, that takes time.

It also takes belief in yourself—not because you're so *unbelievable* but because you believe in the power of God at work in you! He doesn't make mistakes, yet He forgives yours! He sees your sincerity in wanting to do what's right and can arrange favorable circumstances that allow you to be proven trustworthy to your parents and others who are in authority. By relying on God, you become reliable.

Prayer: Heavenly Father, I'm so glad You're perfect and yet forgive me when I'm not! Help me to admit the areas in which I haven't been reliable, and help me do what I can to live up to the trust that others place in me. Sometimes no one seems to have any faith in me or my abilities! Other times they expect too much. Thank You, Lord, for asking of me only what You have enabled me to do. Thank You for showing Your faith in me in Jesus' holy name.

Journaling with God: Do people often trust you too much or too little? Tell God how you feel. Listen for His response.

_____

_____

_____

_____

_____

_____

_____

_____

*I therefore, the prisoner of the Lord,
beseech you that ye walk worthy
of the vocation
wherewith ye are called.*

(Ephesians 4:1, KJV)

Has your pastor ever mentioned "being called" to the ministry? Did you picture the moment as having a Hollywood set with the booming voice of God coming over a loudspeaker?

"Thou shalt preach!" Or perhaps it was quieter—more like a whisper, calling in the night.

Maybe you haven't thought too much about it, but you might have assumed that a calling on one's life comes in a highly dramatic scene, a memorable moment of clear direction, or a stark revelation of the truth. It can! But for many Christians an understanding of their life's work comes more slowly, like a gently rising mist at dawn.

This calling can place you in a pulpit or a cockpit! It can nudge you into preaching, teaching, or reaching to others through social reforms, political influences, environmental protection, or other types of reconstruction. You could be called to write, edit, typeset, or market publications for the edification of Christian readers. You could be called to rear children in a Christ-centered home or a day care center on the needy side of town.

Even if you're unsure of the direction your life's work will take, you can walk worthy of your vocation by making a commitment to pleasing God in every job. If you slap burgers on a grill, you can treat meat with the same standard you'd want someone else to use in cooking your meal! If you greet customers, you can give courteous attention to them instead of the clock or other clerks. If you sell stocks and bonds, you can take stock in honesty and bond yourself to the Lord.

Prayer: Dear God, please help me to have respect for my job, other people, and Your ability to call me so I can hear in Jesus' name.

Journaling with God: List the vocations which interest you the most, and discuss each with God.

_____

_____

_____

_____

_____

_____

_____

_____

_____

_____

Day 81

I have glorified thee on the earth:
I have finished the work
which thou gavest me to do.

(John 17:4, KJV)

Do you still have a job? With your first ninety days at work almost ended, you may find your employer doesn't need you anymore! Cutbacks happen. Layoffs occur. Organizations reorganize, and people get fired.

Sometimes, it's not the person but the position that's no longer needed. Other times, workers just do a lousy job! Either way, the newly *un*employed often feel worthless. They might tell themselves, "See! I can't do anything!"

If your job comes to an abrupt end, you'll wonder what happened and have every right to ask! Maybe you didn't take a warning seriously. Maybe it wasn't your performance but an unworkable attitude that caused trouble. Or maybe you didn't do anything wrong. You just weren't right for this job.

Knowing what needs changing will help you consider your options. If you can correct a mistake or attitude, please do! But just as you need to face the truth about yourself and your job performance, so must you face the lies!

It's a lie to think, "I can't do anything right!" That not only isn't true now, it's a poor excuse that sets you up for future failure. Even if you're tempted to warn others not to expect much from you, such worthless thoughts can make you think even less of yourself. So don't employ them! Instead, be aware that you've apparently finished the job God gave you to do. Unless you're ready for retirement, it must be time for something else! God only knows! So, of course, He's the only One to ask.

Prayer: Heavenly Father, forgive me for speaking against You by thinking worthless thoughts about myself. You created me and gave me experiences, talents, and ability, so that makes me worth something! Please help me to know what I'm to do in Jesus' name.

Journaling with God: Make a list of your special abilities and interests. Thank God for each gift, and ask Him to help you know which are worth the most to Him and also to you.

Day 82

*Commit thy works unto the Lord,
and thy thoughts shall be established.*

(Proverbs 16:3, KJV)

So, what do you think? Have you begun to realize that your unique combination of interests and abilities would fit nicely into a particular vocation? Or do you feel you have a thousand-piece puzzle tossed into a box with no picture to go by on the cover?

If you're in a quandary, trying to envision the work that best complements your abilities, ask a loving parent, sibling, close friend, or co-worker how they see you. Someone who knows you well and *likes* you can outline characteristics which reveal a side of you that's well-suited for a specific job you hadn't yet considered. Or maybe they will sketch in details which clearly show your aptitude for specializing in a wider field you know you like.

Caring people can also paint—*nicely*—the colorful aspects of your personality. For example, they might see you as too "yellow" for door-to-door sales, but sunny enough to greet customers or bright enough to teach!

No one, however, sees you quite as the Lord does! He not only knows who you are now, He knows what you can become with His help. So maybe He wants you to overcome timidity by knocking on people's doors!

More likely, though, God has given you a desire for the very thing He's called you to do. After all, He's the One who gave you those talents and abilities in the first place. He's the One who shapes experiences and opens or closes puzzle boxes for you now. He's the One who sees the picture and brings everything together to help you fit perfectly in Him.

Prayer: Dear God, help me to keep my thoughts focused on You and the work You've established for me in Christ's name.

Journaling with God: Offer to God any thoughts that have distracted you from your work or scribbled over the career to which God is drawing you.

_____

_____

_____

_____

_____

_____

_____

_____

_____

_____

*The Lord works out everything
for his own ends—
even the wicked for a day of disaster.*

(Proverbs 16:4, NIV)

Do you do manual labor? Do you accomplish work with your hands, having clear goals in your mind? Maybe you proofread textbook manuals or edit car maintenance manuals on a computer. Whether you use mental ability or physical agility, God calls you to Emmanuel labor! "Behold, a virgin shall be with child, and shall bring forth a son, and they shall call his name Emmanuel, which being interpreted is, God with us" (Matt. 1:23, KJV).

What a wondrous birth! In Christ came God-with-us Labor: a full-time, anytime job which includes you!

If you listen very long to the world, you might start to think, "God *isn't* with us!" You'll find examples of disaster all around, so you might begin to believe a loving God just couldn't stand by, letting awful things go on forever, and you're right. He can't!

God gave every person on earth a free will and a free choice. Although it breaks His heart to see what people do to themselves and one another, He will not force anyone to turn to Him. So, until Christ comes again to reign, sin will continue to prevail in the world and in the workplaces where people just won't admit God. Without an admission, He might step outside. But that's where you come in!

In any business place, you can make it your place and business to admit God. Even if co-workers slam the door in His face, you're on the inside, remember? God won't barge in, but since you're inside the place, all you have to do is ask Him to come in. Invited, *God is with you*—which will affect everyone else in your workplace. That's Emmanuel Labor!

Prayer: Lord, I was beginning to think You'd been shut out of my workplace, but I didn't realize I could just unlock the door and let You in! Thank You for working toward this end and letting me be included in Your plans in Jesus' name.

Journaling with God: Ask God to bring to your mind specific prayers for your workplace and individuals who come and go.

_____

_____

_____

_____

_____

_____

_____

_____

Day 84

*The appetite of workers works
for them;
their hunger urges them on.*

(*Proverbs 16:26, NRSV*)

Did you know that your co-workers may be starving? They might have three square meals a day or a rounder ten! But if they've spent a lot of time doing work they barely can stomach, a leanness of soul can set in.

Job dissatisfaction generates a famished nation. People soon become listless in work they find unappetizing. They get picky with other employees and bite off clients' heads! They nibble their fingernails with worry, thinking, "I can't stand this job, but the next one could be a lot worse!" They feed themselves baloney!

A work ethnic of hopelessness helps no one. Employees hoard jobs they dislike, keeping them from those who'd eat up similar work! Consider, for example, the sixth grade teacher who couldn't tolerate immature students! When a principal pointed out that sixth graders *are* immature but residents of nursing homes are not, the teacher found a satisfying job. Similarly, people who treat elderly persons as children might consider how their job dissatisfaction does not help the residents of nursing homes feel at home!

When you're discontented, it doesn't necessarily mean you're unhappy with your job. If you've worked long, hard hours or endured lengthy periods of stress, you're probably just tired! Or you could be bored, especially if an entry-level position doesn't challenge you.

If you truly detest your work, talk with God and ask His help in finding something more to your taste. But until He clears a new shelf in your job life, the goal of buying groceries regularly can give you an incentive to keep on working!

Prayer: Dear God, some days I'm tempted to quit my job, even though I don't know what else I'd do. Help me to have at least a taste of Your plans for me in Jesus' name.

Journaling with God: Tell God how you feel about your work. Listen to the solutions or direction He brings to your mind.

_____

_____

_____

_____

_____

_____

_____

_____

_____

Now concerning spiritual gifts,
brothers and sisters,
I do not want you to be uninformed.

(1 Corinthians 12:1, NRSV)

Does your work come in dozens? Did you count dozens of tasks to do, roses to send, donuts to bake, or hours to work?

A dozen tribes of Israelites followed God. Thousands applied, but a dozen apostles accepted Jesus' invitation to keep His close company each day.

As you consider a long-term career, you'll find about a dozen possibilities for ministry listed in 1 Corinthians—give or take a few more listed in Romans. To read those lists yourself, just go a dozen chapters from the beginning of either book.

Seeing the list of ministry gifts helps you recognize the ones God has given you. Although these gifts often come in varying degrees and combinations, you'll find one or two where you have special inclination or interest. For example, you may have a strong gift of discernment which enables you to recognize dishonesty when you see it! This ability also helps you know when someone speaks the truth—a trait parents, personnel managers, and parole officers long to have!

The lists in chapter 12 of both 1 Corinthians and Romans show that each ministry gift comes from God's Holy Spirit, so even a multi-gifted person has no reason to boast. Also, every gift has special value in building up Christ's body, the church. So there's no need for competition since everyone works together toward this goal.

As you learn about the various gifts of the Holy Spirit, you may sense a direction toward Christian service, but don't wonder. Ask! The Giver of ministry gifts can certainly show you how to use His gifts in the very blessed way possible!

Prayer: Heavenly Father, thank You for Your gifts. I'm not even sure what some of them are or what they have to do with me! But I trust You to put on my heart and mind how You'd have me work toward building up the church in Jesus' name.

Journaling with God: As you read Romans 12 and 1 Corinthians 12, list the ministry gifts which God has given you. If you're uncertain, ask Him to help you recall specific incidents relating to each gift.

_____

_____

_____

_____

_____

_____

_____

Day 86

*To one he gave five talents,
to another two, to another one,
to each according to his ability.*

(*Matthew 25:15, NRSV*)

"I don't have any talents!" Oh, yeah?

Although Jesus' parable of the talents refers to money, people have similar attitudes concerning their abilities too.

Unless they're multi-talented, they may fool themselves into thinking they're no-talented! That's what happened to the one-talent guy in the parable, and look where it got him! He wound up losing what he had.

As you evaluate your interests and abilities, you might not find obvious talents, but that's no cause for burial! For instance, you might think you can't sing well because your voice range doesn't shatter crystal, but who needs broken glass anyway? If you can hold a key note for around twenty seconds, your church choir director probably wants to hear.

Other obvious talents include an ability to write a poem or story, sketch a picture, and play a musical instrument or a role in act I, scene I. Television widely broadcasts sports using physical talents from acrobatics to a zooming ski-jump. But it also takes talent to catch a fish someone might eat, build a house someone might buy, deliver a speech someone might hear, or close a sale for something some-one might need. So, please note: *Real talent* goes into help-ing other people.

As you think about the talents you do have, think about career possibilities through which they could be shared. These may influence a future vocation, or they may be areas you can enjoy as a hobby. Either way, you'll be doing what you *like*.

Prayer: Dear God, forgive me for trying to bury the talent You gave me because it wasn't visible! Help me to increase my ability and enjoyment of Your gift by using it with skill as a hobby or career that's helpful to others and pleasing to You in Jesus' name.

Journaling with God: Ask God to help you uncover talents you have hidden.

_____

_____

_____

_____

_____

_____

_____

_____

_____

_____

*The one who had received
the five talents went off at once
and traded with them,
and made five more talents.*

(Matthew 25:16, NRSV)

Have you updated your resumé? Even if you love your job and have no intentions of doing anything else, your company might have other ideas! No one knows what a new management or trend might change. For example, when lamp oil prices became combustible a century ago, who would've expected electricity? That little invention created countless jobs and extinguished others, but the people who saw the coming trend could prepare for it. Prayerfully, you can do the same, especially if you see new technology being developed in your field of interest.

Right now, for example, most businesses have found a use for computers. Photographers crop pictures on a PC; mechanics diagnose engine problems; accountants keep count. At select salons, you can even get a computerized perm! You can also update resumés easily on a computer, inserting dates and places of employment along with a brief description of your work.

As you describe what you do each day, state your primary tasks first, using active verbs in the present tense. Include your areas of responsibility. Then edit your resumé for each interview, mentioning first the aspects of your job that most relate to the one for which you're applying.

For personal references, ask permission to use the name of your pastor, an old family friend, a favorite teacher, or someone else who knows you well and believes in you. Don't be shy about including relevant information concerning awards or recognition in your field. You've already doubled your God-given talents through use! So, instead of belonging only to you, what you have has benefited other people too.

Prayer: Dear God, I haven't yet doubled everything You've given me by sharing it with other people, but I'd like to try. Thanks for showing me where and when in Jesus' name, please help me to have the courage to succeed.

Journaling with God: Discuss job trends with God, and ask Him how you can prepare more or increase your skills.

_____

_____

_____

_____

_____

_____

_____

_____

_____

_____

Day 88

*His lord said unto him,
Well done, good and faithful servant;
thou hast been faithful over a few
things, I will make thee ruler
over many things:*

(Matthew 25:23, KJV)

At the end of ninety days, many employers reassess a new employee's value, not necessarily in dollars but at least good sense. Although a favorable evaluation might not mean a promotion yet, it could mean additional employment benefits including extra cash!

In many workplaces a salary increase at varying time increments may be company policy. But, even if a raise comes automatically at the end of three months, you have now proven your ability to do the job. God knew you could! So, you might want to congratulate Him as you give yourself a well-deserved pat on the back.

Whether you stay in your present place of employment or move to another position, you'll continue to have choices and options throughout your working years. But, as you encounter new and exciting opportunities, don't jump at any chances until you've had a chance to pray!

Eventually, you'll remember. If you forget, God can help remind you that He's there. It's your career, but it's also His. You're His ongoing work for all of your adult life and into eternity too.

No one knows exactly what the future will bring or what obstacles you'll encounter. But, as you continue to place your faith in God, He'll continue to reveal His faithfulness to you. Praise Him! Thank Him! And no matter how far your career advances, always let Him be the One in charge.

Prayer: Heavenly Father, thank You for Your faithfulness in seeing me through these first ninety days on the job. Help me always to see You in my work and life in Jesus' name.

Journaling with God: Is God calling you to a new level of responsibility? Are you proving yourself faithful in little aspects of your job? Talk with Him about these matters.

_____

_____

_____

_____

_____

_____

_____

_____

_____

_____

_____

Day 89

*To everyone who conquers
and continues to do my works
to the end,
I will give authority
over the nations.*

(Revelation 2:26, NRSV)

Everyone wants job security and a guaranteed salary! Everyone wants to get paid. Highly reputable companies may *seem* to offer secure benefits, yet no one can but God!

Your Heavenly Father does not promise that you'll be highly successful. He doesn't guarantee top positions in your chosen field. He doesn't promise you'll be in charge of the company someday, nor does He tell you to expect you'll always have a salaried position—or any position for that matter!

You might find yourself spiraling into a recession, depression, or obsession about your work! You may be over your head, underpaid, and down and out of a job! You might clip enough classifieds in the "Help Wanted" section to fill an industrial waste bin. You might lose count of people who tell you, "Don't call us. We'll call you." You might use an advanced college degree as a placemat for your table. And yet, by keeping faith in God, you will rule nations!

That's a promise! That's job security at the highest level! So you'll want to know what's the catch. God clearly states His conditions. (You didn't think every promise came free, did you?) *If* you conquer . . . what? That depends on you!

You may have to battle pride that says, "I don't need God! I'm doing fine by myself." You may have to face doubts that say, "God has forgotten me."

You must overcome whatever threatens to make you give up—which brings you to the second condition for obtaining God's promise—*If* you keep doing the work He gives you to do. What's that? You know! "This is the work of God, that ye believe on him whom he hath sent" (John 6:29, KJV).

Prayer: Dear God, I don't want to work apart from You. Help me to remain faithful in Jesus' name.

Journaling with God: Ask God to show you the areas in which you need His strength to overcome.

_____

_____

_____

_____

_____

_____

_____

_____

_____

Day 90

*One of his disciples said unto him,
Lord teach us to pray.*

(Luke 11:1, KJV)

Before a job interview, you need some awareness of the company who's hiring or position for which you're applying. You need a general understanding of the products and company goals to be able to ask intelligent, relevant questions. Then you'll get the answers you need—and you'll also show a potential employer your genuine interest in the job!

One of Jesus' disciples did this. When he noticed the time his Master spent in prayer, he had the good sense to ask about it! As recorded in the Gospels, the Lord's answer gave an outline that Christians can personalize each day.

The prayer printed below gives an example of how you can pray—powerfully and regularly—for your work, workplace, and anything you notice that's in need of the Lord's Prayer.

Prayer: Dear Father which art in heaven, let Your name be holy in me and my workplace. Let Your kingdom come and Your will be done in my life. Give me this day all that I need to be nourished in Your Word and Spirit. Forgive my trespasses against You, myself, and others, and help me also to forgive.

Lord, lead me not into the temptation of doubting You or giving up, and deliver me from the evil of ill will at work in this world. Let it not be my own power, but Yours that overcomes. Let Your blessing of me and my work bring glory and honor to You, forever in Jesus' name.

Journaling with God: Congratulations on completing your first days on the job! Although these pages end, your devotional time of Bible reading, journaling, and talking with God in prayer have just begun!

_____

_____

_____

_____

_____

_____

_____

_____

Using a loose-leaf notebook of convenient size, record your daily conversations with God, noting the date each day. As you keep in close touch with the Lord, let Him continue to record His holy heart, mind, and Spirit in you!

God be with you always. And may you always keep up the good work He's begun in you in the name and power of your personal Lord and Savior, Jesus Christ!

_____

_____

_____

_____

_____

_____

_____

_____

_____

_____

_____

_____

_____

_____

_____

_____

_____

_____

_____

_____

_____

_____

_____

_____

_____

_____

_____

_____

_____

_____

_____

_____

_____

_____

_____

_____

_____

_____

_____

_____

_____

_____

_____

_____

_____

_____

_____

_____

_____

_____

_____

_____

_____

_____

_____

_____

_____

_____

_____

_____

_____

_____

_____

_____

_____

_____

_____

_____

_____

_____

_____

_____

_____

_____

_____

_____

_____

_____

_____

_____

_____

_____

_____

_____

_____

_____

_____

_____

_____

_____

_____

_____

_____

_____

_____

_____

_____

_____

_____

_____

_____

_____

_____

_____

_____

_____

_____

_____

_____

_____

_____

_____

_____

_____

_____

_____

_____

_____

_____

_____

_____

_____

_____

_____

_____

_____

_____

_____

_____

_____

_____

_____

_____

_____

_____

_____

_____

_____

_____

_____

_____

_____

_____

_____

_____

_____

_____

_____

_____

_____

_____

_____

_____

_____

_____

_____

_____

_____

_____

_____

_____

_____

_____

_____

_____

_____

_____

_____

_____

_____

_____

_____

_____

_____

_____

_____

_____

_____

_____

_____

_____

_____

_____

_____

_____

_____

_____

_____

_____

_____

_____

_____

_____

_____

_____

_____

_____

_____

_____